GOING COASTAL: SANTA CRUZ COUNTY AND BEYOND

Elizabeth Ivanovich

Published by BookLocker.com, Inc., Bradenton, Florida.

Printed in the United States of America on acid-free paper.

BookLocker.com, Inc.
2014

First Edition

CONTENTS

AUTHOR'S NOTE

All but one of these stories first appeared in the Santa Cruz, California publication **Student Guide** (and its sister magazine **Summer Santa Cruz**) between 2002 and 2014. The final essay, "2001: A Kitchen Odyssey," is taken from the August / September 2008 issue of the now-defunct women's magazine **Moxxi**. (In turn, it was the original version of an essay previously printed as "My Family Has A Wacky Sense of Solidarity," which appeared in the June 3, 2004 Home Forum section of **The Christian Science Monitor**.) All appear with the permission of these various publications, and my deepest gratitude to their editors and publishers!

Most of these selections were written as advances for local events. This led to the dilemma of how to make them "evergreen" enough to warrant inclusion in a book. Some stories were slightly rewritten to include updates, while others required postscripts to describe more dramatic changes over the years. A few made the most sense in their original versions. (All website / contact information was current at the time the book went to press.) The articles appear in chronological order (except for "2001"), but since the chronology is based on the academic calendar, it may seem counterintuitive at first. (For example, winter 2010 comes before spring 2010, because the winter academic quarter precedes the spring one.) While this sequence often causes thematic leaps from story to story, I feel that this approach better reflects the eclectic spirit of Santa Cruz County itself. I hope you will enjoy spending time with the real-life characters of the Central Coast.

PERSONAL ART, COLLECTIVE HEALING
[Adapted from the Winter 2002 Student Guide article]

Since the cataclysmic events of September 11th, 2001, people have struggled to find solace and justice in the midst of overwhelming, often unspeakable grief. How can the visual arts set in motion the healing process, both for the artist and the viewer?

Local artist / teacher Coeleen Kiebert has a unique perspective on this subject, for she has been dealing with these life-altering questions for far longer than the past few months. Since the unexpected death of her son David in Rome in 1996, she has created the Justice Series, a remarkable array of sculptures that explores both the grieving process and Kiebert's personal quest for a just resolution. Like most of us, she found that the events of September 11th were affecting her in unconscious ways.

"[On September 11th] I went to the studio...I was presenting this whole ladder series with these deep divers on them, and the clouds climbing, diving into the depths of the unconscious. But, as I listened to NPR throughout the day on September 11th, the pieces kept wanting to be towers. I kept telling myself 'Don't go there, stay in your own imagery. There are two separate things that are happening.' Several hours later, when I was doing the tops of the towers, they could no longer be the deep divers with the goggles on anymore. By that time, they were representing the souls of the people who died in the World Trade Center, and I had this image of them hovering over the debris of what was happening. This was still on September 11th...I set them aside for about ten days, so they'd be thoroughly dry before I fired them [in the kiln]...Then I turned on NPR again and fired the kiln. When the kiln was matured and cooled down, I opened it up. The pieces had completely exploded...I started looking for the surviving shards of the pieces...I found that the pieces that represented the souls were totally undisturbed, weren't even chipped or nicked. So I took all the shards out, and I decided to back up into the process, and surrender to what is going on, and stay as connected to it as I could, rather than trying to separate out [of it]...in order to learn what we're supposed to learn."

Although Kiebert had mere days to prepare for the 2002 edition of Open Studios, she felt compelled to continue the arduous glazing and gluing of the tower pieces, "not pieces I would ever sell, just as a process thing." As she continued to listen to personal stories of the tragedy, she found that she had more tolerance for this usually tedious process. "It just all seemed very purposeful in a symbolic way. So, I guess it's my own way of having stayed in touch...I think it's really important to stay in touch with what happened and the struggle of the people who went through all that, who are still going through it."

Viewers' perceptions were equally illuminating for the artist. "[The 2002] Open Studios' timing was a gift. I thought it was quite an opportunity to have that interaction of people around the September 11th pieces that I did, and especially around the Justice Series. I think that people are relieved that art can talk about these things...we find it hard to have words to say. One of the best parts of the Open Studios experience for me was the way people were so open and candid with me about things that were happening in their own personal lives that were related; sudden death experiences, great loss experiences, frightening experiences. [The art] becomes symbolic for something we can connect with each other about. Certainly, people weren't avoiding the meaning of the work in any way at all—they really seemed to meet it very fully."

It becomes clear that art can be a remarkable conduit for healing, not only as an expression of intangible feelings but as something that unites us. Different people can have completely different opinions about a single work's meaning and value, but they share the experience of viewing that specific piece of art. For Kiebert, it is an equally important part of the artistic process. "I think that when you do art and are trying to tap into the unconscious, you should be ready for the fact that some difficult material might come up. Then there is the viewer, who is looking at that material...It's a real privilege to be able to do art, to be able to have the imagination and opportunity to develop the skill to do it. So, I think a certain responsibility comes along with that."

POSTSCRIPT: Coeleen Kiebert continues to create sculpture, and is the author and publisher of **All of a Sudden: The Creative Process**, now in its third edition. She teaches ceramic sculpture in her private studio, and through University of California Santa Cruz (UCSC) Extension courses. For more information, visit www.coeleenkiebert.com. Open Studios Santa Cruz takes place during the first three weekends of October each year; consult www.artscouncilsc.org/open- studios for details.

WATSONVILLE TAIKO: ECHOES OF TRADITION
[Adapted from the Fall 2003 Student Guide article]

The Japanese word taiko literally translates as "big drum" or "broad drum." To the Western mind, a big drum evokes an image of pounding aggression. While taiko drumming certainly harnesses power, much of this power derives from subtler factors. Seemingly disparate ideals of tradition and modernity, physical prowess and mental concentration, solitude and community all unite in the pulse of taiko.

As the artistic director of Watsonville Taiko for the past eleven years, Ikuyo Conant approaches these dynamics in several impressive ways. (In a lesser capacity, she is also affiliated with Monterey's Shinsho-Mugen Daiko and Morgan Hill's Sandoshi Taiko.) She teaches taiko classes, composes and arranges taiko scores, writes about taiko and its place in people's lives, and programs and choreographs performances. Her warm manner and uniquely nuanced perspectives make it clear that taiko is far more than the act of hitting a drum.

Taiko has existed in various guises for centuries in Japan. However, the current multi-rhythmic group form, Kumidaiko, was invented by jazz drummer Oguchi Daihachi in post-World War II Japan, and came to the United States in the 1960s. [Conant provides this and other historical information in her 1997 essays "History of Taiko in Japan" and "Taiko in the United States."]

When composing for Watsonville Taiko, Conant considers the tension between the old and new rhythmic structures. "The traditional rhythm has been passed down for such a long time because it's simple. So, it's rather boring. [Laughs] We have traditional music and rhythm, but it's combined with more interesting modern rhythm. The traditional rhythm, we have to interrupt with a modern beat...It's the same music, but if you

4

change an instrument or beat, experiment with different rhythms...It's a challenge. My music is not very traditional—because of the nature of the group, we tend to use a lot of people and it becomes more like orchestral music."

This breaking of boundaries extends to Watsonville Taiko's seemingly unusual collaboration with Santa Cruz Ballet Theatre this past February. "[SCBT director] Robert Kelley asked us, and I like ballet because I put lots of ballet elements in taiko. Not the elements of dancing, but the discipline behind it...In ballet, people learn the basics, and spend ten to fifteen years [honing them]. Then, when it comes to performing, they can combine everything because they are rooted in basic skills. It's the same philosophy I like to apply to taiko."

According to the 2003 North American Taiko Conference roundtable schedule notes, almost half of taiko performers are not of Japanese descent, while half of those are not Asian at all. What gives taiko this multicultural appeal? "I think it's such a basic thing. People want to have something physical as well as mental...I think what's more important is the spiritual journey, not only through taiko drumming but through something else...[this aspect] is so easy to see through other cultures, and they'd probably find the same traditions to be found in their own culture."(Intriguingly, Conant says that the gender ratio of taiko drummers is 60% female to 40% male in the USA, while in Japan the ratio is reversed.)

Newcomers are sometimes surprised by Conant's emphasis on the mental as well as the physical aspects of taiko. "My biggest concern is the attitude of the performers onstage. If a performer is not focused, it's very hard to keep the sound together...People come and hit [the drum], but based on the mental level, you don't get any energy...That's the part we really have to cultivate. It's not really the drumming technique, but more the mental part that people need to learn. People don't realize, they think "Boom! Go over there and...bap!" but it's more how to make that energy inside yourself, how to express that energy using drums. That's very different."

Since Watsonville Taiko is a nonprofit organization, it serves many different functions for its participants as well as its audiences. Some members of the group have no desire to perform publicly at all, concentrating instead on their personal interactions with the instrument and the people in the group. Some people's goals change once their skills develop, while others simply wish "to make life easier with good rhythm," as Conant was once told. For her, all these approaches are welcome. "The purpose of the discipline is not to become a great performer, but to become a decent human being, to understand other people's needs and ideas, and your differences. That's the whole purpose of drumming."

POSTSCRIPT: Watsonville Taiko averages thirty public performances per year, in staggeringly diverse settings. These include relatively intimate occasions such as weddings and funerals, as well as huge events like the Big Sur Marathon. Having celebrated its twenty-second anniversary in 2014, Watsonville Taiko maintains its dizzying schedule of performances, as well as classes and workshops. (Those wanting more information should visit www.watsonvilletaiko.org.) Ikuyo Conant has served as artistic director of the organization since 1992, leading the group's ear-pleasing and eye-opening convergence of East and West.

GO AHEAD, MIX IT UP!
[From the Spring 2003 Student Guide]

Imagine the ability to control the programming on your favorite radio station for ninety minutes straight, commercial-free. Picture a perfect soundtrack that enlivens road trips, parties, and long evenings of studying. You can even create a heartfelt serenade to your beloved--one that can last for years, and can be listened to again and again. All this will cost no more than a dollar or two. Does it sound like a far-fetched pipe dream? Not a chance! Happily, these are just a few of the joys of the homemade compilation tape.

(A brief semantic note here: people refer to these tapes in one of two ways. Some call them mixed tapes, as in tapes that compile a mixed assortment of songs. Others call them mix tapes, since they feature a unique mix of particular songs. In this article, I will use the latter term, since most tapes I've encountered unite songs in a thematic way. However, the terms are often interchangeable, and to my mind equally correct. Now, then...)

The wondrous mix tape has a multitude of uses. If your friends are sick of hearing about how great your favorite bands are, you can compile a tape of all their best songs and prove your case, possibly converting your pals in the bargain. (The more devilish music fan can use it to start arguments. Who sings the better version of "Molly's Lips," Nirvana or the Vaselines? Is the original version of Beck's "Devil's Haircut" preferable to its various remixes? Put them all on a tape, play it for the passionate music fan in your life, and let the debates begin!)

Out of curiosity, I e-mailed some of Santa Cruz, CA's rock luminaries and asked about their experiences with mix tapes. Each had strong opinions about what songs and styles should be included on a tape, and uniquely personal memories of tapes they had heard.

For Mikala Clements, singer / bassist for Here Kitty Kitty, mix tapes have a nostalgic quality. "[They] bring back such memories of junior high and high school—[of] sitting on the floor with different albums lying around, figuring out what songs to use and what order to put them in."

While some tapers like to put similar genres together throughout a mix, the consensus among these respondents is that diversity and variety is best. Jon Cattivera, singer / guitarist for Time Spent Driving, clarifies the point: "I like the tapes to be somewhat diverse, but it's the songs that matter the most—no matter how similar."

As for specific song selections, each respondent has personal favorites. Mikala Clements asserts, "Any mix tape I ever made had at least one Violent Femmes song on it." While Lesterjett singer / bassist Alexi Glickman admits that he doesn't think he's ever made a tape, his would include tracks by Jackson Browne, the Beatles, the Pixies, Arvo Part, Weezer, the Strokes, Aphex Twin, and Radiohead. Jon Cattivera sent a full track listing of twenty-six songs, encompassing everything from Social Distortion to Smashing Pumpkins, from Coldplay to Johnny Cash.

Those wary of combining wildly divergent musical styles on a tape can take heart. It's possible to come up with a theme that ties them all together. Often this theme has to do with something personal rather than the songs involved. Jon Cattivera says, "I made a mix tape for a girl who I worked with. She gave me a hard time for being a vegetarian, I gave her a hard time for smoking cigarettes. I made her a mix tape called 'Vegetarians and Cigarettes.' Later, she became my girlfriend of four years."

Each respondent has a vivid memory of a mix tape used as a token of love, which comes as little surprise. At once inexpensive and deeply personal, mix tapes are great flirtation devices. The shy suitor can be assured that it's the music--not the person--who is doing the talking. Still, this indirection can sometimes cause uncertainty. Alexi Glickman explains: "The first gift I got from the girl I'm crazy about was a mix tape. It was this amazing funk / soul kind of thing, but I was crushed when I got to 'The Thrill Is Gone.' It ended up that she hadn't been trying to tell me anything."

When it comes to mix tapes and love, Mikala Clements' story of a boyfriend's tape tops them all. "We had been dating for a few months and he gave me a tape of great songs. I remember listening to it and making my oldest sister listen to it over and over again. He liked me, he really liked me!" Clements' boyfriend must have chosen some excellent songs indeed, for he is now her husband.

What other object can bring hours of listening pleasure, start conversations and friendships, and (if all goes well) be the catalyst for true love? I hope that this article has given you the inspiration to start making a mix tape of your own. Be careful, though...this sort of thing could easily become an obsession.

POSTSCRIPT: While the advent of the recordable CD (and later, the USB flash drive) turned this into a historical piece fairly quickly, the cassette still holds a place in many music lovers' affections. The San Francisco Mixtape Society accepts all three formats at its events, but has been known to reserve special perks for those who submit an actual tape. While I use CDs as often as cassettes, I find vindication in the fact that compilations are often called mixtapes (as a single word, no less!) to this day, regardless of format.

After reading this article, a friend phoned me to protest. "You would never put all of the remixes of 'Devil's Haircut' on the same tape, or put a song and its cover version together." This is true. In my defense, I never meant to suggest that people should do such things, only that they could if they wanted to. Ahem...

Following the demise of Lesterjett, Alexi Glickman played in the Botticellis and toured with Little Wings. He continues to perform in the Bay Area in various guises, most recently releasing the album **Fourth Dementia** under the name Sandy's. Mikala Clements has stepped out of the public eye to help run her family's Scarborough Lumber locations, and is store manager of the Scotts Valley Scarborough Lumber Ace Hardware. Time Spent Driving reunited in 2012 after a seven-year hiatus, and Jon Cattivera and company have completed an album due for release in late 2014.

IT'S MUSIC, IT'S COMEDY...IT'S SECOND CITY!
[From the Winter 2004 Student Guide]

On February 20th, 2004, Second City will grace the Rio Theatre stage with its renowned sketch comedy. The troupe's touring company will feature six performers, a stage manager...and a musical director. Why would comedic actors need a musical director? As it turns out, music has been integral to Second City since its 1959 inception. Not only does music underscore comic sketches and fuel funny songs, it greatly shapes the company's performance philosophies.

Beth Kligerman, a senior associate producer for Second City, has been with the company since 1993. This gives her a unique perspective on how music affects the troupe's style. Kligerman shed light on the process by phone from Second City's Chicago headquarters.

While singing is not required in a Second City audition, the group's revue-style performance format means that everyone deals with music. This includes those actors who don't consider themselves singers. Kligerman elaborates: "In a revue, the opening number, maybe 70 to 80 percent of the time here at Second City, is a musical number. So, even if you have never sung before, you come here and have to sing. So you're flexing a muscle here that you might not elsewhere...If you are a singer and audition for a musical, that's a given. But if you come to Second City, you might be asked to write a song, or...if you don't write a song, you're still going to be exposed to actually having to sing that song, whether you're a singer or not."

The musical director wields an unusual amount of influence in Second City, often unconsciously. As Kligerman points out, even resolute non-musicians rely on the musical director to help establish a sketch's tone. Because so much relies on improvisation and collaboration, live musicians are always

11

present in a way that they generally aren't in scripted productions. "So, even if someone wasn't musically inclined...that person would [be influenced] just by having the musical director in the room with him all the time, or, in the case of the touring company, in the van all the time. The musical director will be listening to music...or playing music, or as another outlet...performing elsewhere. So...you're being influenced in a way that you might not be normally."

The standard for musical excellence is set high for all involved. In his memoir Days and Nights at the Second City, co-founder Bernard Sahlins explains that this results in good comedy as well as good music: "If you...sing badly in an opera parody, what is the subject of fun? Really, your own lack of skill. Since we are using parody as a vehicle to carry a message, it must be done with some skill lest the lack of skill become the message."

This emphasis on craft has led several Second City alumni to blur the line between comedic acting and mainstream musical performance. Take former Second City Toronto performers Catherine O'Hara and Eugene Levy. Having played folk singers in the hit film A Mighty Wind, they participated in well-received concerts in character at rock venues (such as the Warfield in San Francisco) during 2003. A better-known example is when former Second Citizens Dan Aykroyd and John Belushi created the Blues Brothers.

Beth Kligerman is not surprised by this. "I think there is a clearly distinguished, strong link between people who come from here...[including] people you wouldn't think necessarily could sing or understand music. Look at Horatio Sanz, who on **Saturday Night Live** probably only has to sing twice a month—he wasn't hired as a singer, they don't do that, right? But they know he's got the skill to sing. When he was here at Second

City, he used his talent and ability to sing in different ways...He's got a wonderful voice, so he uses it."

Kligerman is equally enthusiastic about Second City's current musical climate. "There's a gal at Second City by the name of Nyima Funk...if she were not doing this [stage] work right now, she should have a record deal. Her husband, who works for us, also has a great voice. They work with one of our musical directors, and the three of them have this band on the side called the Grits. [Nyima]'s an amazing singer, so when she writes a song... it just brings down the house when she opens her mouth, whether or not the song is hysterically funny."

Kligerman concurs with Sahlins' belief that "writing a funny lyric seems easy but is very, very difficult." Part of this has to do with the need to establish a coherent scene within a short song. "There are premises and characters, depth of character, and arcs to the story that have to be told in three minutes. That's pretty darn difficult." Happily, this alchemy does happen. Kligerman speaks fondly of former troupe member Paul Dinello's "The Jesus Song." "It's just a great guitar song about how a guy by the name of Jesus stole [Dinello's] girlfriend...It's amazing just to see someone pick up a guitar and sing satirical songs." Kligerman is audibly proud as she concludes: "It's an amazing accomplishment. Funny music is a great thing."

MORGANI'S WORLD
[From the Winter 2005 Student Guide]

If you walk down Pacific Avenue on a Sunday afternoon, you're likely to see him. He makes 120 appearances a year at various venues, assuming a different persona each time. He will appear as a life-sized Oscar statuette, or Uncle Sam. He can be seen in head-to-toe sequins, or an outfit covered in duct tape. He prefers to perform with his face and body completely covered, which adds to his air of mystery. This masked man plays an accordion, and is known as the Great Morgani.

Do you find all this rather confusing? Imagine how Frank Lima, accordionist and creator of the Great Morgani, must feel. "Sometimes I feel there's Frank Lima the ex-stockbroker, and there's this wacko case called The Great Morgani. And it's okay, as long as the two don't talk to each other. Frank Lima the stockbroker is a very conservative guy, and Morgani is the completely out-of control performance costume thing. Just two different individuals."

Like most legends, the Great Morgani had humble beginnings. Lima received his first accordion at the age of nine, when a door-to-door salesman visited his parents' home in Santa Cruz. "In 1951, every kid played the accordion," he notes, ruefully adding "Then Elvis came along in 1955 or '56, and no kid would be caught dead with an accordion!" While the young Lima couldn't foresee the arrival of Elvis, he already had a touch of rock-and-roll rebellion. "I took lessons for a couple of years, then they kicked me out because I wasn't reading music...I could hear a song a couple of times, and it would stay in my head."

Today, Lima has a repertoire of 1,291 songs, all learned by ear. "I don't know how I know them...they just run from my head to the fingers to the accordion...Trouble is, I know how to play the songs, but I forget that I know them unless somebody

14

mentions the songs. My head's full! It's magic. If I ever get hit on the head, there goes a career. So, I gotta take care of these things." He categorizes his songs according to country of origin and subject matter. Still, the question nags: with such a wide range of music in his head, does Lima ever get outrageous requests from his listeners? Do hecklers pester him with demands for Lynyrd Skynyrd's "Free Bird"?

Lima grins. "Well, actually, I learned 'Free Bird' and [Led Zeppelin's] 'Stairway To Heaven.' I wanted to play ['Stairway'] on my own terms, so I turned it into a French waltz. It's beautiful! I like it when I play the Dell Williams area [of Pacific Avenue], and the motorcycle guys across the street go 'Hey, accordion guy, play "Stairway To Heaven"!' It just blows 'em away."

Needless to say, Lima's unorthodox approach occasionally rankles the accordion players' community. "I showed up at an accordion meeting six or seven years ago in [San Francisco]. Very conservative, an older crowd, very predictable. I showed up in black sequined platform shoes, Groucho-nose glasses, black beret, my accordion covered in black with the nameplate from an Electrolux vacuum cleaner on the front...they were not amused." He insists that his antics stem from a real love of performance, not disrespect for his instrument. "You've got to have a sense of humor about [the accordion]. I'm not putting it down—if anything, I think I'm putting me down. I'm having fun with the instrument."

Lima hit upon the costuming idea eight years ago as a way to stand out among Santa Cruz's street performers, having no idea of how far it would go. "[The costuming] is just out of control. I keep pushing it more and more...It's just become this whole integral art form. But that's what I enjoy." Even so, showmanship can be a double-edged sword. "Music ends up in kind of second place to the costumes. But I'm still an accordionist first. I don't want to say, 'I'm a costume designer playing the accordion.'"

Eventually Lima hopes to release a coffee-table book, tentatively titled **The Creative Madness of Morgani**, which will feature photos and stories about his 150 costumes and innumerable concerts. Ideally, the book would be accompanied by a CD or DVD of his performances, but music licensing problems may make that difficult. In any case, Lima takes his musical legacy in stride.

Twenty years from now, when I can't hold this [accordion] up anymore, I'd love to have [today's] 10-year-old kid [grow up to] say 'I remember the guy who used to play, and wore those funny costumes!' That'd be a great legacy. I'm the end of the family name, I'm taking all this madness with me." Morgani devotees find that hard to believe. Lima laughs, "[Community TV videographer] Peter McGettigan said, 'Frank, you'll still be downtown in 30 years...they'll have a hologram of you [playing] as they're passing by!' Who knows?" Indeed. After all, in Santa Cruz lore, Frank Lima is already immortal.

For performance or booking information, phone Frank Lima at (831) 423-3800 or visit thegreatmorgani.com.

POSTSCRIPT: Lima released his book, entitled **The Great Morgani: The Creative Madness of a Middle-Aged Stockbroker Turned Street Musician**, in 2007. In February 2014, Lima announced that he would no longer perform in downtown Santa Cruz, due to the stronger enforcement of recent city ordinances that restrict activities such as street performance. There was a prompt public outcry on social media and in the local press. In May 2014, the Santa Cruz City Council moved to alter the legislation. Designated performance areas are being developed, but Lima has called the proposed spaces "constrained and rigid...not compatible to any kind of performance." As of

September 2014, the matter remains in limbo, while Lima continues to perform elsewhere in the county.

SIX TOP PICKS OF '65 HITS
[From the Spring 2005 Student Guide]

I approached this 40th anniversary theme issue with caution. Not only do I consider nostalgia to be a dangerous exercise, I wasn't alive during the era in question. So, I examined the list of the top 100 songs of 1965 skeptically. Happily, the list proves that the concept of "oldies music" is a relative thing. To be sure, 1965's Top 100 had a disproportionate share of novelty records (such as Shirley Ellis's "The Name Game") and a few ill-advised cover tunes. (Why would people opt for the Searchers' uptight take on "Love Potion Number Nine," when the Clovers' original version is such a slinky treat?) But, on the whole, these songs have aged extremely well. Below are some of my favorites from 1965's Top 100 list, and the reasons why they are so timeless.

THE BEATLES, "Ticket To Ride": The Beatles enjoyed unprecedented popularity in 1965 with the film **Help!** and a wildly successful tour. Luckily, "Ticket To Ride" stands on its own merit, beautifully evoking the mixed feelings involved in a romantic breakup. The opening couplet "I think I'm gonna be sad / I think it's today, yeah" perfectly captures the numb ambivalence brought on by a relationship's end. The lyrics wisely leave things unsaid, allowing the music to provide the song's true emotional core. George Harrison's chiming guitar arpeggios shimmer with melancholy, while Ringo Starr's surprisingly tough drumbeats contribute a sense of half-repressed anger. With all this heartrending splendor storming behind them, John Lennon and Paul McCartney refuse to give in to treacly impulses. Their closing falsetto shouts of "My baby don't care!" sound downright gleeful. In the end, it's this dark-humored touch that gives hope to the brokenhearted.

THE KINKS, "All Day and All of the Night": Ray Davies' distinctive, somewhat nasal voice sneers and growls in true punk

18

fashion, years before punk was born. With such a powerful vocal performance fueling the song, people tend to forget the brilliant guitar work contributed by Ray's brother Dave. (As you'll see here and in the Beach Boys entry below, there was a lot of sibling revelry going on in the 1965 music scene.) Dave Davies' charging, clanging guitars add a fuzzy menace to the song, influencing many garage and metal guitarists in the process. Meanwhile, Mick Avory's shuffling snares and popping kick-drums lend a chugging groove that wouldn't be out of place in '70s glam rock. "All Day and All of the Night" predicts four musical genres within two minutes and twenty seconds. It's a new land-speed record!

THE ZOMBIES, "Tell Her No": Colin Blunstone's warm, sonorous voice is one of the British Invasion's greatest gifts to pop music. His rich tone contrasts gorgeously with the grittier voice of keyboardist / songwriter Rod Argent, bringing tension and depth to the song. (This dual vocal melding of toughness and beauty would become a hallmark of '70s power-pop.) Argent's jaunty keyboard work serves as a cruelly ironic counterpoint to the quiet pain in Blunstone's vocal. The payoff comes when Blunstone whispers the lyrics "And if she should tell you, 'I love you' / Just remember, she said that to me." Where many singers would descend into hysteria, Blunstone's restraint is nothing short of devastating.

SAM THE SHAM AND THE PHAROAHS, "Wooly Bully": Admittedly, it's disconcerting that Domingo "Sam" Samudio sounds remarkably like Adam Sandler as he sings this song. (How a 1960s rocker can evoke a current comedian is spooky indeed, but a question for another time.) In a strange way, that fits right in with "Wooly Bully"'s goofy charm. From the shambling chord changes to the wobbly note in its honking saxophone solo, "Wooly Bully" sounds like it's ready to collapse at any time. It's not the chaos of incompetence, but the chaos of fun, that you hear. (This rollicking playfulness is what I miss most in today's overly produced hits.) The band shouts indecipherably, and Sam bellows "You got it, you got it!" And so they do.

JAMES BROWN, "Papa's Got A Brand New Bag (Part 1)": It's incredibly difficult to explain James Brown's brilliance in words on a page (though Roddy Doyle comes close in his novel The Commitments), but I'll try. Where Sam the Sham succeeds through entropy, James Brown shows the genius of the lock-step arrangement. The loping bassline, choppy guitars, and insistent horns are perfectly balanced, punctuating each other without overstepping their bounds. As a result, James Brown can let loose vocally without overwhelming the groove that his equally talented backing musicians lay down. There's so much going on musically, yet the record feels uncluttered and spare, urgently perfect.

THE BEACH BOYS, "California Girls": The symphonic introduction melts into a warm bass line, which gives way to simmering horns. Mike Love's lead vocal balances his usual swagger with the underlying sweetness of Brian Wilson's lyrics. Love's conversational tone lulls listeners along, so that they are completely knocked out by the Wilson brothers' gorgeous harmonies during the chorus. The second verse's "ooh-wahs" have a strangely hymnal sound, adding weight to what could have been a breezy, sleazy ode to girl watching. In spite of the Beach Boys' sunny reputation, there's an aching character to their arrangements that really stands out here. Prefab Sprout's Paddy McAloon once sang that "some things hurt much more than cars and girls." "California Girls" proves that for Brian Wilson, this is not the case.

Several other songs are worthy of inclusion. (Sam Cooke and Junior Walker were just two of the artists I reluctantly left out!) Perhaps it's time to leave it up to you, the reader. Go ahead, dig out your vinyl records or charge up your iPod. When you do, take a minute to consider the sheer scope of popular music, the great records that endure forty years later, and the music lovers who came before us in 1965.

Want to know more? Check out "The **Billboard** Top 100 For 1965," at http://billboard.com/archive/charts/1965.

THE CATALYST: MORE THAN JUST A NAME
[From the Fall 2005 Student Guide]

Many phrases could describe the Catalyst nightclub in Santa Cruz. Pacific Avenue fixture. Performance venue for touring and local musicians. Magnet for Santa Cruz residents and visitors of every stripe. Yet, only one of those three phrases has always held true. The Catalyst began life as a small, co-operatively run Front Street coffeehouse in 1966. However, even in its far different early days, the fledgling establishment would soon embody the lifestyle of Santa Cruz.

The Catalyst evolved as the brainchild of the Consumer's Co-operative of Santa Cruz. Despite its stodgy name, the Consumer's Co-op was a deeply eclectic group of people. Members came from the town's medical, political, legal, and educational communities. [For a list of names, see the introduction of **Catalyst** by Eric Strayer, Gregory Lavin, Marilyn Emery, and John Tuck, Santa Cruz: 1975. Publishing information and page numbers are not specified.] It was chaired by Byron Stookey, who served as assistant to the chancellor of the newly opened University of California at Santa Cruz. While UCSC had no official hand in the co-op or the Catalyst, the university nonetheless would play a pivotal role in the fate of both entities.

UCSC librarian Stan Stevens was also the co-op's treasurer at the time. He explains: "Byron Stookey...urged [the co-op to open] a coffee shop or something like that, because the students didn't have any place to go. There was nothing on campus." Indeed, when the campus opened in September of 1965, the students had to live in trailers while Cowell College was being completed. Since the campus atmosphere was in flux, Stookey felt that the UCSC students should at least have a chance to avail themselves of Santa Cruz's downtown experience. "They could have entertainment and socialize. So," Stevens concludes, "we finally decided to have a coffee shop."

The Catalyst opened on April 10, 1966, managed by the co-op's Al and Patti DiLudivico. The co-op members threw themselves into the coffee house's operations, often finding ways to suffuse the most mundane tasks with the group's idealistic aims. Stevens smiles, "I drove up to San Francisco every month for [American Civil Liberties Union] board meetings. We had a VW van, and I'd go to the Catalyst and load up with pickle barrels, drive up to San Francisco, and leave the barrels off at the pickle manufacturer's. After the meeting I'd go back, and they'd have these barrels filled up with pickles. I'd bring them back to the Catalyst....Of course, the VW van reeked of garlic and whatever goes into the making of pickles! Quite aromatic."

While music defines today's Pacific Avenue incarnation of the club, it was more of a sideline in the beginning. Headlining rock acts performed at the Barn in Scotts Valley; the Catalyst's small space and elderly neighbors dictated more low-key entertainment. Once the Catalyst opened its ballroom after its expansion, dances would take place. For now, one or two musicians would provide quiet accompaniment to the coffeehouse's conversations and activities. The Catalyst patrons themselves, it seemed, were the real draw.

The Catalyst became like Santa Cruz itself, reflecting the town's free-spirited ethos and its capacity to change. Stan Stevens points out that before the UCSC / Catalyst era, Santa Cruz was considered a "sleepy backwater" with one of the largest senior citizen populations in California. "[When] UCSC and Cabrillo came--opening at the same time, essentially--[they] attracted

a much more liberal clientele. Not only students, but faculty and staff...it really changed the social and political fabric of the town. I'd say the Catalyst, true to its name, was where it was all happening. It was pretty wide open."

Happily, the non-elitist Catalyst welcomed the senior citizen, the hippie, and everyone in between. In 1966, historian Carolyn Swift was a Watsonville teenager who often cut her Cabrillo classes to spend time at the Catalyst with new friends from Santa Cruz. One day, she got a surprise. "There I am, going down there to meet all my friends and spend the whole day skipping school...and there's my mother! I'd walked in on my mother from Watsonville, and her church prayer group. All these women had gone to Santa Cruz to the [Hip Pocket] bookstore, and [then to the Catalyst] for coffee. It was the last thing I'd expected to see. Here was my new hangout, my new life! That was what a feature [the Catalyst] was, how different, how unusual. It's really hard to think about now, but it was very new for older people to have this little bit of San Francisco [coffeehouse culture] creep down into Santa Cruz County!" Even today, there is audible amazement in her voice. "All these little old ladies from the All Saints Episcopal Church—I thought they were little old ladies, they were in their forties—were all down there having coffee, having a great time, looking at all the weird people."

The Catalyst building itself compellingly blended the old and the new. It occupied the historic St. George Hotel, which had been a Santa Cruz landmark since 1897. A small corridor separated the Catalyst from the Hip Pocket bookstore, which carried everything from bestsellers to the latest countercultural literature. Although it was discouraged, Stan Stevens confides, "You could go through the little opening [between the Catalyst and the Hip Pocket] if you knew how." This quirk of architecture made the building a one-stop shop for the curious intellectual.

The St. George property boasted an opulent glass door and very thick, bouncy wooden floors. Stevens and Swift both single out the wooden floors as a defining feature of the place's character. Stevens laughs, "When you walked into that place, you weren't necessarily walking on a stable environment to start with! The wooden floor had the typical spring action of an old wooden floor. That aspect of it had a good feeling." This sense of buoyancy gave an infectious verve to the whole venture. The glass door and walls, meanwhile, added a seductive mood of their own. Swift enthuses, "It was just remarkable. You knew that you'd walked into the past...It rained a lot, so you had this wavy glass. To me, it was wonderful."

Expansion, ownership changes, dissolution of the co-op, and relocation would bring dramatic changes to the Catalyst over the next few years. Yet, the 1966 original holds a definitive magic for those who went there. Carolyn Swift notes, "The year 1967 seemed a long way away. We didn't think of hippies as we did later, because it was so new. We only knew that we were eighteen, and this was a lot of fun...Later, about 1970, I stopped going there. It wasn't the same kind of place...It changed, and I couldn't even tell you how."

The Catalyst is located at 1011 Pacific Avenue, Santa Cruz. To learn about the shows at its current incarnation, visit www.catalystclub.com or phone (831)423-1338.

CABRILLO'S HARMONIC CONVERGENCE
[From the Winter 2006 Student Guide]

Imagine an elite chorus of singers, able to perform everything from Beethoven's Ninth Symphony to American spirituals with grace and style. Respected Czech music critic Dr. Olga Kittnarova has called the group "inspirational." The vocalists have ardent fans in Moscow, Prague, and St. Petersburg. The Latvian-Canadian composer Imant Raminsh has chosen them to premiere his latest masterwork. Where would you travel to find such a group? Boston? New York? Perhaps, but you don't have to. You can go to Cabrillo College in Aptos to enjoy these remarkable voices, led by Cheryl Anderson.

Anderson joined Cabrillo's music faculty in the fall of 1991. Today, she oversees four of the six choral groups on campus. Her expertise in genres ranging from opera to modern music, augmented by her warm demeanor and distinguished teaching background, has gone a long way toward the success of Cabrillo's music program. In person and via e-mail, Anderson explained the unique joys and challenges that come from pursuing music in a collegiate setting.

While the Cabrillo Symphonic Chorus and the Cabrillo Chorale are geared toward Cabrillo's music majors, Anderson's other campus choral groups, Cantiamo! and the Cabrillo Youth Chorus, also involve community participation. Membership requirements, however, are no less stringent for the general public. Prospective singers in any choral group must be able to sight read music, produce certain depths of vocal tone, and understand the nuances of ensemble work. Since each chorus has a slightly different niche, Anderson notes that most singers choose to join more than one choral group.

How does Anderson foster this versatility? "Since we are an educational institution, I try to design the literature to meet the needs of the singers, as opposed to looking at it from the point of view of selling tickets...We vary the literature for all the groups by style, period, form, language, and composer. It makes it profoundly interesting for me, and it keeps us all on our toes and engaged. There is no lack of choral literature. History has provided us with an incredibly rich legacy of brilliant works."

Anderson is especially committed to the Cabrillo Youth Chorus and its ideals of encouragement and education. In an era where music courses are mercilessly cut in schools, the Youth Chorus provides a rigorous, exciting challenge for young voices. These youthful charges are more than qualified for the task, as Anderson learned when several teenaged members joined the Cabrillo choral groups' tour of eastern Europe this past summer. "It was fabulous, because the more experienced singers, in terms of years, got to watch these kids behave as well, musically, as anyone else. The way they accepted responsibility on the trip and demonstrated themselves as young women...I kept thinking, 'I was never like this when I was 15!' They were just wonderful."

If you missed this acclaimed European tour, don't despair. The choral program records CDs of all concerts, and several have been released recently. The Symphonic Chorus offers **Music For The Feast of Christmas**, while Cantiamo! presents its **Concert For A Winter's Eve**. At press time, the Cabrillo Youth Chorus had a still-untitled release in the works. These albums are available for sale at the groups' performances, or through the websites listed at the end of this article.

The Cabrillo choral department's spring fundraiser is a typical combination of wit and expertise. On March 25th, all the Cabrillo musicians will participate in "Bach Around The Clock" from 10 a.m. to 10 p.m. Honoring what would have been Johann Sebastian Bach's 321st birthday on March 21st, the event features a choral performance of Mass In B Minor, among other works. Anderson enthuses that it will be "incredibly fun" to celebrate Bach, and welcomes this rare opportunity for interaction between the choral groups. With its equal emphasis on art and craft, the choral program has a bright, epic future ahead. "Our music majors continue to cycle through a very strong system which is maintained by brilliant community singers." Anderson notes that the groups have sung at national choral and educational conferences, which she considers an important and inspiring part of the program's outreach. She has her eye on a potential choral performance at Carnegie Hall sometime in 2007, with other travels on the horizon as well. At any rate, she and her students will continue to take full advantage of their musical opportunities.

"I'm incredibly lucky to live my dream job. We can sing the full gamut of great music... Basically, I want us to be a world-class choral program, able to address any music from any style. To do that requires musical literacy, top vocal ability, a desire for growth, and a willingness to devote one's self to the art."

POSTSCRIPT: The Cabrillo Chorus performed at Carnegie Hall in June 2007. In 2009, the chorus performed **Messiah** in Dublin, Ireland to commemorate the 250th anniversary of Handel's death. Cheryl Anderson continues to lead the various Cabrillo choral groups, and works with the Santa Cruz Symphony as a choral director and guest conductor. She is also the music director of the First Congregational Church of Santa Cruz. For more information about choral group performances and auditions, visit the Performing Groups sidebar at www.cabrillo.edu/academics/music.

CELLULOID HEROES
[From the Spring 2006 Student Guide]

As a filming location, Santa Cruz has long attracted Hollywood directors. The town's scenery has marked films as diverse as 1971's **Harold and Maude** and 1987's **The Lost Boys**. Today, Santa Cruz is no longer a pawn in the Tinseltown game, but a mecca of homegrown cinema all its own. At the forefront of this evolution is the UCSC Film and Digital Media department.

While Film and Digital Media did not become an official campus department until 1998, it has produced successful filmmakers throughout its existence. Alumni include Academy Award-winning film editor Stephen Mirrione, and acclaimed documentary filmmaker Graham Rich. Graduates have gravitated toward independent filmmaking, with particular success at the Sundance Film Festival. Given UCSC's maverick reputation in academia, is this niche encouraged in the classroom?

Department chair Chip Lord concurs that the department has a somewhat different approach than most film schools. "We have more access to hands-on and instructor feedback about filmmaking than most undergraduate programs...In our production classes, students tend to wear all the hats of production rather than specializing in any one technical area." While this may fit naturally with the "do-it-yourself" ethic of indie cinema, he insists that the department is not emphasizing a certain filmmaking style. "I think our outlook is more aligned with 'independent' rather than 'Hollywood' [movies], but our film studies cover all facets of American and international cinema."

Current UCSC film production major Jade Fox worked on Solomon Burbridge's short **Phase 5,** which was screened at Sundance in 2004. She proclaims, "One of the strongest assets of the Film and Digital Media department is the emphasis on culminating well-rounded students." Fox feels that the curriculum's emphasis on critical analysis and theory does much more than foster scholarly knowledge. It "cultivates a strong sense of social, political, and historical relevance and, thus, expression." With UCSC's emphasis on versatility and a strong directorial vision, it seems natural that Film and Digital Media graduates would be well-received by Sundance.

2003 Film and Digital Media graduate Cam Archer is skeptical regarding any natural affinity between UCSC filmmakers and the Sundance Film Festival. "Sundance is as much an enigma as the average UCSC film major, no?" Archer originally graced Sundance with his short **Bobbycrush** (which was nominated for a Student Academy Award in 2004). This year, he returned to the festival with his first full-length feature, **Wild Tigers I Have Known**.

In spite of the fact that he had attended two years earlier, Archer felt unprepared for the intense scrutiny at this year's Sundance. "I was a nervous wreck, more so than ever before. Having a feature there—it's scary...Gus Van Sant, who is an executive producer on the project, showed up for the premiere screening. So the pressure was on."

Archer's UCSC experience may have prepared him for the industry fishbowl in unexpected ways. "I found [the film program atmosphere] to be pretty competitive, though I don't know if other UCSC film majors would admit that. Looking back on it, it seems ever more obvious now." Professor Lord provides evidence for this, noting that out of 500 majors in the department, about 100 of them have applied for and been accepted into the film production concentration.

Fox, a graduate of City College of San Francisco, sees UCSC's approach as more welcoming and innovative than the stereotypical film school's curriculum. "For prospective film students, UCSC is not just an alternative to the highly competitive [film schools including] UCLA, but often an intentional choice due to UCSC's grounding in activism, dissension, and subversion." Since the school attracts unique and ardent viewpoints, it makes sense that these would be reflected in students' film work. "Due to this ideology, UCSC draws and produces great visual artists and storytellers," Fox enthuses.

As Film and Digital Media program evolves, it adapts to the changing world of cinema. Professor Lord notes that the department has eliminated the use of 16-millimeter film thanks to the continued improvement of digital technology, and reveals the impending addition of a Ph.D program. With its combination of technical mastery and distinctive passion, one thing becomes clear: Independent or mainstream, with or without the Sundance Film Festival's accolades, the UCSC Film and Digital Media department's horizons are unlimited.

For more about the UCSC Film and Digital Media program, visit http://film.ucsc.edu.

POSTSCRIPT: Professor emeritus Chip Lord retired as department chair in 2010. His work continues to be featured in exhibitions worldwide, and he was honored as part of a campus film symposium in June 2011. Cam Archer's most recent release is the documentary short **Their Houses** (2011). He is working on his third feature film, the documentary **Practical Life**. Jade Fox lives in the greater Los Angeles area, and currently works as a freelance commercial production manager.

SANTA CRUZ VINYL: CUTTING A GROOVE
[Adapted from the Fall 2006 Student Guide]

I confess: I am a vinyl record fanatic. (I even refused an iPod one Christmas.) Santa Cruz is the perfect place to feed a vinyl addiction, or to nurse a new one. Via e-mail, I asked the proprietors of downtown's record shops to explain what makes vinyl so irresistible, and how digital music has changed the landscape for Santa Cruz's record lovers.

LOGOS BOOKS AND RECORDS
1117 Pacific Avenue
(831) 427-5100
www.logosbooksrecords.com

Logos has been a Santa Cruz fixture since 1969, long before the iPod or the CD. Owner John Livingston notes that the store originally stocked 33 rpm vinyl records, mostly used. "New records had become very competitive price-wise in those days, and the [profit] margins were so small that we never felt it was worth handling them to any real extent." The store broadened its variety of used music formats (though it eschewed 8-track tapes in favor of the cassette), creating an enthusiastic audience of buyers and sellers.

The compact disc's arrival changed everything. "What we figured was that the CDs would keep us in business for the general market, and we would maintain a smaller but well-chosen section of vinyl for collectors and those who still preferred that medium. This is exactly what happened." Classical music buyers especially embraced the CD; until recently, vinyl held appeal only for nostalgics and collectors.

While Logos has suffered an overall drop in music sales in the past ten years, vinyl sales have risen somewhat. "The collectors' market has burgeoned, prices have gone way up and people are willing to pay them, and some young people have taken to vinyl." Logos hopes to continue expanding its vinyl inventory, although "many artists sell well in CD but not at all in vinyl." Livingston feels that downloads will hasten the CD's downfall: "Access to the [digital] sources is too great, and anyone can burn discs as they choose." He predicts, "CDs will gradually disappear."

STREETLIGHT RECORDS
939 Pacific Avenue
(831) 421-9200 or (888) 648-9201
www.streetlightrecords.com

Since its 1997 arrival, Streetlight has been known for its strong CD selection. Manager Roger Weiss admits, "Some people don't even know we carry vinyl." While the stereotypical Streetlight vinyl buyer is a "male between the ages of twenty and fifty," others also seek the format. Deejaying still relies on vinyl, so many Streetlight customers scour the electronica and rap sections for breakbeats and samples. Furthermore, Weiss explains, "We get our share of collectors looking for expensive early pressings, as well as folks just looking for whatever version is available."

Streetlight stocks an equal amount of new and used vinyl, though many opt for a lower-priced used record over new. "Price is always a factor; everyone's looking for a bargain." Weiss notes that the perceived notion of quality differences between new and used records can be wrong: "not all audiophile [vinyl] is new, and not all new vinyl is of audiophile quality." Ultimately, vinyl buyers "simply prefer the [audio] fidelity over CDs. So, regardless of whether it's available on CD, they covet the wax."

Since Streetlight has multiple locations, how do Santa Cruz's patrons differ from their San Jose and San Francisco counterparts? Weiss explains that due to their larger populations, those cities contain more vinyl enthusiasts. "Santa Cruz does, however, do better with punk vinyl than the other locations," he adds, and "supports reggae vinyl more."

METAVINYL RECORDS
320 Cedar Street
(831) 466-9027
www.metavinyl.com

Metavinyl opened as Metamusic Records in digital-happy 2005, yet is devoted exclusively to vinyl. (The store generally stocks new releases that are unavailable used, as well as recent re-releases that would have been prohibitively expensive in their original pressings.)

Owner Jonathan Schneiderman proclaims that vinyl records provide full aesthetic satisfaction for the listener. "For the nostalgic, vinyl brings people back to a bygone era...when listening to music was a full audio, visual, and educational experience," he asserts. "The liner notes were read thoroughly and the sleeves examined fully in addition to the music. Moreover, vinyl is still the finest audio reproduction method known to the consumer. Record grooves reproduce analogue sound; [digital] does not."

As tactile objects, vinyl records appeal to the serious music fan as downloads never will. "To purchase a record is to buy a tangible item. To download a song or burn a CD is not. People recognize this, and many will agree that if true ownership is desired, a record is the item to be purchased. To have an MP3 of one's favorite song is simply not good enough."

So, put down your MP3 player and sift through the record bins downtown! You may find unexpected treasures. It's a great way to absorb the distinctive character of this music-loving city.

FAST TRACK FOR SLOW WAVE
[From the Spring 2007 Student Guide]

Conventional wisdom proclaims that your course of collegiate study will steer the rest of your life. This can make choosing a major agonizing for creative people with a technical knack. Do you starve in a garret, or become an office wonk for The Man? The choice is between art or practicality, the heart or the head. Right? Wrong. Cartoonist and UCSC graduate Jesse Reklaw proves that with a little ingenuity, you can have it both ways.

Reklaw first displayed a flair for computer programming in 1992, as an electronics student at Cabrillo. He says via e-mail, "It was totally inspiring! I found that I loved abstracting problems, and piecing together solutions on the computer." As Reklaw's technological prowess flourished, he still enjoyed drawing and painting. "In 1993 I enrolled at UCSC, with a double major in CIS [Computer and Information Science] and art (my focus was acrylic painting, though I got to do some comics in independent study). The computer arts lab at Porter College was a great resource. A classmate and I started UCSC's first student art gallery on the web."

Reklaw asked friends for stories to draw, and became particularly intrigued by their dreams. These dream-related strips became the focus of Reklaw's new comic, **Slow Wave**. "After I graduated in 1995, I was interested in both comics and the web. I guess it's natural that I started **Slow Wave** as a webcomic." He solicited reader submissions on his site, and soon the dream stories were coming from all over the world. One of the very first webcomics, Slow Wave flourishes more than eleven years later, long after most Internet enterprises of the era have come and gone. (Slow Wave also appears in print in various alternative newsweeklies.)

While Reklaw has been an innovator in online comics, he refuses to abandon traditional methods of publishing. "There's something magical about paper and about tangible art and books. I don't think I could ever do without them," Reklaw asserts. "I'm often inspired to make zines, collages, and other physical objects. Real materials are often more relaxing to work with, though digital arts and digital publishing can be exciting, with their ease of use and room for innovation."

One of Reklaw's traditional zines, **Couch Tag**, features stories taken from the author's life. The second issue's "Thirteen Cats of My Childhood" demonstrates how Reklaw's succession of hapless pets figured into a youth plagued by frequent moves and strained family relations. The story was chosen for the 2006 edition of Houghton Mifflin's **Best American Comics** anthology. "I've known the series editor, Anne Moore, for a few years. So I was able to personally submit the story to her, and she told me she liked it right away. But I was still shocked and happy to be accepted," Reklaw says. The acceptance was especially meaningful to Reklaw as a fan as well as an artist. "The guest editor, Harvey Pekar, has been a big influence on my comics career, so I was thrilled that he liked my work."

The **Best American Comics** inclusion brought Reklaw new concerns as well as new opportunities. It's one thing to publish a personal zine and distribute it to a few hundred people, but now "Thirteen Cats of My Childhood" would reach a much larger audience. Would his family be upset by the more widespread exposure of such sensitive material? "I was a little worried about them being angry, but it's also very refreshing for me to put that stuff out there," Reklaw notes. "In some ways, it's made it easier to talk about these family issues that have been ignored for so many years. It's weird, but I find it easier to make a story about a personal issue, publish it, and give my dad a copy, than it is to bring up the topic just between us."

The anthology brings Reklaw's art and family life full circle in another strange way. "When I was in high school, my father enjoyed Harvey's **American Splendor**, and decided to make a comic book of his own life. He paid me $10 / page to draw stories that he later published. I was only 17, and this was my first paid art job; maybe without it I wouldn't have even become a cartoonist. So, I have Harvey to thank for that. When I was at a signing for the **Best American Comics** in Seattle, I gave Harvey a copy of my dad's comic."

Reklaw is philosophical about the possibility of commercial success, doubting that his audience has changed much since the **Best American Comics** release. Even so, he has tentative plans to release a five-chapter memoir (including "Thirteen Cats") sometime next year. "I've always wanted to do longer comics stories. Even though strips are fun, they can be limiting,, so I'm glad to have this opportunity." He has an eye toward other projects as well: "Some are loosely based on my life, but none will be autobiography. One book about me is enough, maybe too much!" Perhaps Reklaw shouldn't rule out another memoir just yet. After all, keeping his options open has certainly served him well so far.

POSTSCRIPT: In 2009, Reklaw announced that **Slow Wave** would be shifting toward a continous-narrative webcomic format. This was prompted in part by dwindling advertising revenue for alternative newsweeklies (which had begun to drop their comics as a result), and partly from a fear that fresh material was lacking. The artist has published **The Night of Your Life: A Slow Wave Production** (Dark Horse, 2008) and **Couch Tag** (Fantagraphics, 2013) since the **Student Guide** article originally appeared. Prints from his sketchbook project, **LOVF**, are for sale at slowwave.com/LOVF/index.html.

SINGING THE BLUES
[Adapted from the Spring 2007 Student Guide]

The Santa Cruz Blues Festival evolved shortly after local blues club Moe's Alley opened in 1992. Bill Welch and his other Moe's Alley partners noticed the absence of festivals in Santa Cruz's otherwise vibrant musical scene. "It's usually slow [for the club] in January, February, and March, so we decided to start a festival [to work on] during those slow months and have something to build the interest up in Santa Cruz," Welch explains. The first Santa Cruz Blues Festival took place in 1993, featuring an eight-act bill headlined by Albert Collins and Jimmie Rodgers. "We had a one-day event, and sold it out. That doesn't usually happen in the first year for festivals. You have to learn from your mistakes, and we were lucky enough to have such a great, rabid fanbase of people in Santa Cruz who came out to the festival the first year." As the festival grew, so did its core of support. In May 2014, the festival celebrated its 22nd year at Aptos Village Park.

Welch admits that he had no idea the festival would become so successful when it started. "We definitely carved out a niche. Santa Cruz is just a very unique market. People support the arts, and music is part of the arts, in our eyes at least. It's really a credit to the people who live here, who support us year in and year out, who trust our judgment as far as the artists [we present]."

Since the festival has a single stage, there is nothing to distract from the performances. Welch and his cohorts strive to draw the biggest and best blues acts to the festival, most of whom would not normally play in Santa Cruz. This staggering parade has included the Neville Brothers, Little Feat, Gregg Allman, John Lee Hooker, Buddy Guy, Robert Cray...the list goes on and on. "Lots of artists just didn't have a place to play here [before], because the venues weren't big enough for them," Welch says. The Blues Festival bookers study radio request information and look at other festivals to determine who would be a good match, but enthusiasm plays the biggest role in choosing performers. "One fun thing about doing the festival is being able to book it and pick out bands you really like," Welch confides. "I don't think we've ever had a bad act at the festival...We never fell prey to anybody booking something we didn't really like. We've had that luxury, to promote music we really love."

The Santa Cruz Blues Festival has a built-in draw for artists: its location. One of Welch's favorite moments each year is bringing performers to the area and showing them Aptos Village Park. "Lots of times, when you're on tour, you don't have a choice of places to play: auditoriums or stadiums, places not really that beautiful," Welch says. "Aptos Village Park has backdrops of oak trees and redwoods. It's just stunning, green, and pretty, especially on Memorial Day weekend when we've been lucky to have great weather each year. The flowers are blooming, and the ocean's just a mile away."

Welch muses that the festival has not changed much over the years, though he aims for subtle enhancements. "We've gotten a little finer-tuned each year...If someone has a bad time at the festival and has a comment, we try to address it and improve upon it each year." The Blues Festival event staff numbers several hundred, and each person is committed to the process. "It been kind of a fun event to do each year, but it's a very labor-intensive event also," Welch notes. "It's not like it's something we put up in one day and take down...It's definitely a labor of love, heavy on the labor!"

What about the future of the Blues Festival? Welch vows to keep going as long as the process stays enjoyable and Santa Cruz audiences remain supportive. However, he can't predict what will happen to the Blues Festival musically. "If you look at the artists we've [had] over the years, a lot of them have passed on." Collins, Hooker, Charles Brown, and Ray Charles are just a few that Welch mentions. "There are not a lot of first-generation blues guys around. It's an American style of music that's ever-changing. So, I have no idea who'll be there, whether it'll be Jonny Lang or Keb' Mo' or who actually rises to the occasion to be the next blues star...There are some gaping holes in the blues world, but there are always some great musicians coming up." You can bet that once the new blues legends come up, they'll be coming up to Aptos Village Park to headline the Santa Cruz Blues Festival.

The Blues Festival lineup was being finalized after press time. For up-to-date schedule and ticket information, visit www.santacruzbluesfestival.com or phone (831) 479-9814.

ART ON WHEELS
[From the Fall 2007 Student Guide]

Picture an intricate, multicolored mosaic made from thousands of Mardi Gras beads. Visualize a laser light show created with neon sticks and side-lit tubing, or a model of the entire city of Seattle, Washington, built to scale in miniature. Most would agree that these visual works are labor-intensive in their own right. Now, imagine that the mosaic, light show, and model do not occupy a canvas or the center of a room, but instead cover the surfaces of working motor vehicles. Welcome to a world where aesthetics and mechanics collide to produce one-of-a-kind objects known as decorated cars, or ArtCars. From September 15 through November 25, the Santa Cruz Museum of Art and History will pay tribute to these creations in its exhibition **History of the Decorated Car: Things That Roll Series**.

"Using cars as a medium is typically a bigger commitment," explains Bay Area artist Philo Northrup. "The car itself costs thousands of dollars. On top of that, the artwork needs to be weatherproof, impact resistant, and able to go 55 mph without incurring the wrath of the local DMV. It usually takes years to make, so even the most prolific ArtCar artists usually make less than ten over the course of 20 years." Since the creation of an ArtCar is a demanding, sometimes isolating process, Northrup and longtime Santa Cruzan Harrod Blank felt the need to give their fellow ArtCar creators opportunities for critical kudos and public interaction. Blank and Northrup presented their first annual ArtCar Fest in 1997, and organize decorated car visits to schools and hospitals year-round.

ArtCars are not the product of a specific artistic movement. Rather, they come from a diverse group of individuals who may have little in common otherwise. Some ArtCar creators live in major cities, but many hail from rural communities with little funding to support the arts. Visually striking ArtCars have come from taxi drivers, furniture makers, homemakers, and postal carriers (as well as from traditional sculptors and visual artists). Even so, exhibition curator Susan Hillhouse warns against the temptation to view these artifacts mainly as folk creations or outsider art. "True, some of the ArtCar people are not professionally-trained or professional artists. However, there are a number who have studied art and who make their livings through art sales or art education. I think what draws these people together is the process of creating beauty and surprise out of the mundane, as well as the sense of community created by the sharing of the process and the 'product.' It is fun; it can be somewhat obsessive; it sometimes serves as therapy."

In the introduction to his book **Wild Wheels** (Pomegranate, 1993), Blank reveals that his first ArtCar was an outlet for his adolescent romantic frustrations. Others have created ArtCars to work through grief, overcome alcoholism, or cope with conditions such as insomnia and schizophrenia. Is this therapeutic benefit what draws people to the complicated ArtCar process?

Hillhouse notes, "I think it can be a benefit of making art in general. I know that some, but certainly not all, ArtCar artists created their vehicles out of trauma or strife."

Northrup has his own theory. "It's not only that some ArtCar artists have no artistic training. Some have no external support whatsoever for being creative. America is a nation of merchants, and the population generally lives without art, so for someone in this environment (e.g. Simi Valley, CA; Marcola, Oregon; Seale, Alabama), it may sometimes take a catalyst (e.g. a tragedy) to take the courageous plunge to wear your heart on your sleeve."

This comforting quality spreads to those who view the ArtCars as well as those who create them. Who wouldn't smile at the sight of Albert Guibarra's **Hippomobile** or Jackie Harris's **Fruitmobile** on an otherwise dreary highway? For the ArtCar to cast its practical magic, it must always be a fully functional vehicle. "That is part of the deal," asserts Hillhouse. "To make a decorated vehicle and then undecorate it is a life style; to decorate a vehicle and drive it as such is a way of life. ArtCar artists have a way of life. Otherwise, it is not a car, it is a precious sculptural object. ArtCars can convey messages and they can create interactions with people who may never meet otherwise. ArtCar creations invite communication and therefore extend community. This attitude or value of the ArtCar being a moveable vehicle creates this community on a daily basis."

As striking as photographs may be, they could never portray the full glory of the ArtCar. To remedy this, the museum will sponsor its own equivalent of the ArtCar Fest on September 29. From 11 a.m. to 4 p.m., viewers will find one hundred ArtCars parked along the intersection of Pacific Avenue and Cooper Street in downtown Santa Cruz. A selection of artists will be on hand to talk about their creations. A fashion show and live music will round out an event sure to excite the most jaded local art patron.

Hillhouse knows that museum visitors will embrace the ArtCars. "Santa Cruz is an interesting community. There is so much creativity here, so much openness to the creative impulse that this very democratic style of art fits well into the aesthetics of the community. As Harrod says, 'An art car is often a fantasy made into reality, a symbol of freedom, and a rebellious creation. Not only does an art car question the standards of the automobile industry, but it expresses the ideas, values, and dreams of an individual.' Does that not sound a bit like Santa Cruz?"

For much more about the ArtCar phenomenon (including pictures), go to www.artcarfest.com.

STICKS AND STONES: THE PHILOSOPHY OF INSULTS

[From the Spring 2008 Student Guide]

Insults can be shouted from stages or mumbled under your breath. They can make you laugh when spoken in a movie's scene, or cry when muttered by someone you love. The most effective ones tend to be no more than a few words long. Yet, any insult, whether clever or just cruel, is actually a complex statement that reveals as much about the insulter as the one who is insulted. UCSC humanities professor Jerome Neu explores the whole phenomenon in his new book, **Sticks and Stones: The Philosophy of Insults** (published in November 2007 by Oxford University Press). Via e-mail, Professor Neu shed some light on the complicated nature of this topic.

STUDENT GUIDE: What inspired you to explore the subject of insults?

JEROME NEU: Like everyone, I've suffered my share of slights, slurs, and even abuse—of disappointed expectations of attention and respect. The compelling issue is just how sensitive, and how forgiving, to be. And here an understanding of the nature of insult (of just what it is that makes something wounding), and of relevant norms and conventions can be of some help. Of course, those who are closest to us are in the strongest position to disappoint, and the problems of how vulnerable to be (insofar as that is in our control) become most troubling in relation to them.

SG: What was your most unexpected discovery in the process of researching and writing **Sticks and Stones**?

JN: To insult is to assert or assume dominance, either intentionally claiming superiority or unintentionally revealing lack of regard. (It is an important fact that insults can be unintentional—more a matter of negligence or thoughtlessness than willful malice.) The power play can in any case be serious, and when considered psychoanalytically may be understood as deeply rooted in anal erotism ("Up yours!"). This connects with the large place of sexuality in the language, gesture, and subject-matter of insult. But spelling this out needs argument (interested readers might start with the chapter of **Sticks and Stones** entitled "Assault from the Rear").

SG: Before now, I had never really considered the ambiguity involved in what makes an insult an insult. The insulter's intent, the insultee's experience and perceptions, and other outside factors are just a few variables. Do you think society has reached a consensus on what insults always "hit below the belt," or are things becoming more and more relative?

JN: Certainly there is no consensus. Don Imus ran up against the ever-shifting standards when he lost his job last year for his witless, racist, and sexist slur against the members of the Rutgers women's basketball team. This came after he had had a lengthy and successful career of wide-ranging and often equally witless insults. While standards are shifting, and often contested and inconsistent, I would not call them "relative." They are often enough quite clear (as with the "n-word," at least when used by non-blacks and in unlicensed contexts). Celebrities and politicians generally remain fair game, as are all those "public figures" subject (since the Sullivan case) to higher standards to prevail in libel actions.

SG: In more performative styles of insults—rap battles, heckler / comedian exchanges, the dozens—do you think the prime objective is to insult the opponent, or to gain the respect or appreciation of the onlookers / audience?

JN: Public insult contests are just that, contests. The path to victory is through insulting one's opponent, but the aim is honor and glory. The interesting phenomenon has to do with what turns a ritual insult into a personal insult, a game into a fight.

The context of joking and play can often defang what would otherwise be biting insults, but lines can be crossed. I explore in my book some of the ways in which framing conditions can fail.

SG: How has the Internet affected the nature of insults? On the one hand, there's relative anonymity. Then again, a flame war or blog post can be archived indefinitely or shouted down by thousands of offended people at a time (rather than one or two). Do you think people are becoming more shameless or more chastened?

JN: One effect of the Internet has been to preserve and disseminate some insults that might otherwise have sunk without notice. Written statements used to be more widely preserved than spoken ones. But since the coming of cell phone and digital camera videos and the YouTube effect, things have changed. (Ask former Senator George Allen of viral "macaca" fame.) The Internet offers a new format and a new forum. And, as you suggest, the Internet provides a screen of anonymity that emboldens some. But then, even without anonymity, the speed and ease of digital communication encourages some to let the flames flare.

SG: One Amazon.com customer wound up his review of **Sticks and Stones** by praising the number and quality of insults that the book will add to the average reader's repertoire. Does this worry you at all?

JN: Not at all. Satire and sometimes even crude abuse can be valuable. (Sometimes criticism is appropriate.) The resources for insult are vast, and clever and imaginative insults can have an independent pleasure of their own (even if we are the target). From Shakespeare, to Rostand's Cyrano, to Camille Paglia (a modern master of vituperation), verbal fireworks can amuse and enlighten. Of course, not all insults are merely verbal, and words (contrary to the schoolyard chant about "sticks and stones") can wound.

For more information on **Sticks and Stones**, visit the Oxford University Press webpage at http://www.oup.com.

POSTSCRIPT: Neu continues his work as a Distinguished Professor of Humanities at UC Santa Cruz, affiliated with the philosophy and psychology departments. His book **On Loving Our Enemies: Essays in Moral Psychology** was published by Oxford University Press in 2012.

ONE MAN'S TRASH, ANOTHER MAN'S...GUITAR?
[From the Fall 2008 Student Guide]

What do a Millennium Falcon toy, a washboard, a toilet seat, a tire, and a shovel have in common? Most people would answer, "Absolutely nothing." If they visited the Felix Kulpa Gallery in downtown Santa Cruz, they would respond differently. There, they would find a permanent display by local artist Robbie Schoen (who also operates the gallery four days a week). For more than ten years, Schoen has fashioned discarded objects like these into elegant, whimsical guitars with the full capability to rock.

One day Schoen was driving on the Highway 280 exit in San Jose, when he spotted a catalytic converter on the shoulder of the road, its exhaust pipe still attached. "It spoke to me, and said "Take me home and string me. I'm a guitar'...I don't suffer from inanimate objects speaking to me all the time," he chuckles. "This was just so obviously a beautiful thing, I had to have it. I pulled over, picked it up, and took it home." This converter became **Wreck & Roll**, the first electric guitar Schoen made.

Schoen firmly believes in chance and inspiration, yet is not precious about his artistic process or products. "It's not a thing where I think, 'Here's a bass I made from a toilet seat that's black, I'm going to make a guitar with a toilet seat that's white.' It's aesthetic, and based on what necks I have, and switches...It's not that thought out, it doesn't need to be." Still, while some aspects of the work can be changed at the last minute, others (such as drilling holes for strings) are strictly regimented. Different objects come with their own advantages and complications in the building process, so each guitar dictates its own timetable. Schoen's first shovel guitar took one day to make, but other guitars may need weeks or months of tinkering.

It may seem odd that Schoen's calling involves the creation of musical instruments, given that he is a visual artist with no musical background. "I have to just kind of accept my limitations and be okay with that, that I'm not [a musician]," he admits. "I'm the one who makes the guitar." While this fact may complicate the process a bit, Schoen makes it clear that the guitars are not just for show. "These are real electric guitars that musicians buy, and they play them. Musicians are very fussy. They don't like it if it's just a sculpture. They want the strings, they want the sustain, all these technical things they want...What I do is, I make it for them." When Schoen needs to perfect the musical aspects, he turns to a friend (who has repaired guitars for thirty years) to finish the technical specifications. Musician acquaintances will sometimes test the guitars and provide advice (as well as necks and parts from old instruments).

Local musician Isaac Frankle has become identified with Schoen's guitars. He has played the shovel guitar in concert on several occasions, and sometimes goes by the nickname Shovelman. Via e-mail, Frankle outlines some of the advantages the shovel guitar provides. "The shovel's got some amazing percussive qualities. Since it's metal, I can drum on the body, sample [and] loop the drum part, then lay down a bass line and compose songs over it all," he explains. "Since there's no fretboard, I use a slide to give it that Delta blues sound. I have always considered myself one of the many preeminent surrealist-folk superheroes of our time, and so the shovel guitar was just perfect for me." Frankle adds, "Bustin' out the shovel is a great way to silence a rowdy bar on a Saturday night. They don't know whether to scream or throw hay around!"

Schoen himself is occasionally unprepared for people's reactions to his guitars. He fondly remembers one day when he and a friend went to San Francisco, and Schoen's van broke down near China Basin. "So I took the skateboard guitar with me, and I pulled her around on it, so she wouldn't have to walk everywhere. When we got to the ballpark area, people were just in awe of the thing. People wanted to touch it, wanted to hold it...We sat it in a chair while we were hanging out [in a nearby restaurant's bar], and people would come up—'I'm sorry to interrupt you, but can I talk to you about that guitar?' It just kind of did something, lightened everything, made a connection in a lot of people."

More connections are likely to be made in April, when the Santa Cruz Museum of Art and History will feature twelve of Schoen's guitars as part of its **Notes From Santa Cruz** exhibition. The artist is visibly proud of his instruments' place in local lore, drawing parallels between his varied guitars and the vibrant coexistence of differences in the city. "It shows an eccentricity. They're all kind of eccentric, fun, and bring a smile to your face."

The Felix Kulpa Gallery is at 107 Elm Street, Santa Cruz (next to the back entrance of Streetlight Records at 939 Pacific Avenue). Phone (831) 421-9107 for information. To learn more about Isaac Frankle's music, go to
www.facebook.com/isaac.frankle or
www.myspace.com/isaacfrankle.

THE CALIFORNIA ACADEMY OF SCIENCES LIVING ROOF
[From the Winter 2009 Student Guide]

When the new California Academy of Sciences building opened in San Francisco's Golden Gate Park in September 2008, it instantly became the gold standard for green design, earning the highest possible rating from the U.S. Green Building Council. Some features are glamorous, such as the 60,000 solar cells installed to provide energy. Others, like the recycled blue jeans that serve as wall insulation, are more down-to-earth. Even so, the Academy's most impressive combination of form and function is not inside the building at all, but on top of it. Academy architect Renzo Piano collaborated with environmentally-minded scientists and artisans to create the ambitious landscape simply known as the Living Roof. Plants, skylights, rocks, and wildlife cover four-and-one-half acres of space, turning this roof into an environmental powerhouse.

"The domes, steepness of domes and scale make the Academy's roof the most complex living roof ever built," notes Paul Kephart, CEO and principal of Rana Creek Living Architecture and Nursery, based in San Francisco and Carmel Valley. "We were faced with two main challenges." The Academy's roof would have the steepest slope of any living roof to date, and so it would be difficult to prevent plants from slipping off the roof's rolling hills. Soil-retention modules were needed, but up to that point, they had never been made without toxic plastics. If used on such a large scale, they could singlehandedly crush the Academy's goals for a green roof environment.

To solve these problems, Rana Creek developed special plant trays for the Academy project. Instead of plastic, they use sustainably-grown coconut husks and tree sap from a cooperative enterprise in the Philippines. The coconut husks provide a stable base as plant roots weave through the tray, then completely biodegrade as the plant continues to grow. An astonishing 59,000 of these trays were made for the Academy roof, in order to house 1.7 million individual plants.

The next step was to choose the plants that would go into the roof trays. Piano's aesthetic requirements called for neat, low-growing green plants, while Kephart wished to promote biodiversity within urban environments. The solution involved plants native to California; not only would these not require artificial irrigation, they would provide a safe haven to native wildlife. Kephart experimented with twenty-nine different plant species at Rana Creek's Carmel Valley nursery before choosing nine ideal finalists for inclusion in the roof. Beach strawberries, self heal, and sea pink would attract a wide variety of native birds and insects. Stonecrop, poppies, and miniature lupine would provide nectar for bees and butterflies. Goldfield plants would attract insects beneficial to the ecosystem, while tidy tips would serve as a natural pest deterrent. Finally, California plantain would host endangered butterfly larvae.

How would the Academy keep two-and-a-half acres' worth of plants watered in an environ-mentally sound way? The roof is designed to absorb as much as 3.6 million gallons of water per year (about 98% of all storm water, according to the Academy), so providing the water would not be the problem. The trick, then, was to minimize water runoff. Kephart explains, "The Academy has a very complex drainage and water reuse system as well. Eighteen thousand gallons of water are stored beneath the Academy and filtered before being infiltrated into the aquifer, so we developed a gabion system of interlocked metal baskets with rocks to take the roof's overflow water to the subflow to prevent waste." This way, excess water would be recycled back into the park's system. Not only would this conserve water, it would prevent any pollutants in the runoff from contaminating the Academy's ecosystem.

The Living Roof is not just a marvel in itself; it benefits the entire Academy's operation. Its seven layers of ground cover insulate the building, reducing any need for soundproofing and air conditioning. The roof averages 40 degrees cooler than a standard roof, which helps to prevent the huge building from causing an "urban heat island effect," a potential (if currently unproven) factor in global warming. Skylights let in sunlight and ventilation, lowering energy costs while helping to maintain the Academy's coral reef and rainforest ecosystems underneath the roof.

Since the Living Roof is currently the pinnacle of green design, it's hard to fathom that it may just be a taste of the environmental marvels to come in the future. "Although the most complicated roof built to date, this project is only embryonic in terms of technology," Kephart reveals. "The next frontier involves integrated building systems that support life, that are metabolic and that combine nature with building function." In the meantime, we can cherish the California Academy of Sciences building, a green masterpiece from top to bottom.

The California Academy of Sciences is located on 55 Music Concourse Drive at Golden Gate Park in San Francisco. Call (415) 379-8000 or visit www.calacademy.org for more information. To learn more about Rana Creek Living Architecture and Nursery, visit www.ranacreek.com.

SANTA CRUZ: SOUND AND VISION

[Originally titled "Santa Cruz: Musical Diversity at its Best" in the Spring 2009 Student Guide. The census figure mentioned has been updated from the original story.]

While Santa Cruz's population is just above 60,000, its music scene rivals those of much larger cities. You can find rock, punk, country, blues, reggae, folk, and world music in a variety of settings, from the cavernous Civic Auditorium to the cozy Cayuga Vault. The excitement is not confined to Santa Cruz's city limits: Watsonville's Mello Center, Henfling's in Ben Lomond, and the Cabrillo College Theater in Aptos are just a few of the county's excellent venues. Despite music's deep imprint on the area, no local museum has presented a major exhibition about it. This will change on April 25, when the Santa Cruz Museum of Art and History will offer **Notes From Santa Cruz** and **Compositions: Contemporary Artists.**

Notes From Santa Cruz, curated by Frank Perry, examines music's role in Santa Cruz County life over the past 150 years. **Compositions: Contemporary Artists**, curated by Marla Novo, features current local artists' depictions and interpretations of musical themes. The two exhibitions will appear side by side in the museum's Solari Gallery, and Novo affirms that they were designed to complement each other. "Being an art and history museum, we like to take a subject and interpret it from those two disciplines," she explains. "So yes, the idea of two exhibitions sharing the same gallery space was something we wanted to explore from the beginning; this is definitely a collaboration between the history of music in Santa Cruz with a contemporary art component."

Notes relies on an astounding variety of memorabilia, including sheet music, instruments, recordings, and photographs. It features a strong technological aspect as well, showing the evolution of music-playing devices in its "From Edison to iPod" section. (There will even be sound samples available of the local hits from each musical era.) Yet, when asked about his favorite piece in the exhibition, Perry offers a decidedly low-tech choice. "I like the scrapbooks. The Museum has in its collection a number of scrapbooks that were kept by local musicians in the late 1800s and early 1900s. These preserve photos, programs, articles and other memorabilia that provide a unique window into these people's lives. The scrapbooks are almost like diaries. They help tell the kind of 'people stories' that bring an exhibit to life."

While the county had a strong love of music from its inception, Perry feels that its unique musical character really took shape once UC Santa Cruz and Cabrillo College were established in the 1960s. The influx of students brought variety and new ideas to the population, and the academic atmosphere and new musical facilities encouraged experimentation with sound. (Of course, even the finest musical mind will languish without proper nurturing, which is why Notes devotes an entire segment to some of the county's most beloved music teachers.) "What makes Santa Cruz distinctive is its diversity," Perry states. "The musical diversity is more like that of a larger city."

Indeed, Santa Cruz boasts a staggering variety of musical genres and places to hear them being played. So, it makes sense that **Compositions** employs divergent artistic approaches to portray this atmosphere. "I picked artists who work in different media to make a really rich and exciting exhibition," Novo explains. "For instance, Robbie Schoen has created these great assemblage guitars; Carlos Dye works in ceramics; Pete Saporito has documented local bands through his photographs; and Chris Tedesco, a glass artist, is producing new work for the exhibition." While Novo finds it difficult to choose a favorite piece, she singles out **Skateboard Guitar** by recent **Student**

Guide interview subject Schoen: "You're not sure if you want to ride it or play it!"

Santa Cruz, in its art and its music, has always championed the unexpected. Whether it's the fusion of musical genres or the union of unlikely forms and functions, our artists and musicians will find a way to make them work. "Santa Cruz has always embraced innovation, and music is no exception," Novo says. Perhaps that is why our locale stokes the imaginations of faraway musicians as few others do. Think of Boston indie-rock legend Jonathan Richman's rollicking ode to the Boardwalk's Giant Dipper, "Roller Coaster By The Sea," or Irish band The Thrills sighing "Santa Cruz (You're Not That Far)." Novo agrees, "We are fortunate that this area has attracted big-name and not-so-big-name artists to perform here throughout the years. From high school music teachers to reggae and metal bands, Santa Cruz County has inspired many people to pick up a guitar, enjoy some tunes and bask in this area's uniqueness."

WHERE THE WILD THINGS ARE
[From the Winter 2010 Student Guide]

In a career spanning over 60 years and more than 100 children's books, Maurice Sendak has crossed the line from beloved children's author to cultural icon. He has received the National Medal of Arts, as well as the Library of Congress "Living Legend" medal. Playwright Tony Kushner and **Wicked** author Gregory Maguire have written entire books in appreciation of Sendak. With all this acclaim, it can be difficult to consider Sendak's complex, sometimes unsettling work on its own terms. Philadelphia's Rosenbach Museum and Library, holders of the world's largest Sendak collection, decided to present an exhibition that would place his portfolio into context. **There's A Mystery There: Sendak on Sendak** debuted at the Rosenbach in May 2008 to coincide with Sendak's 80th birthday. The exhibition is now running at San Francisco's Contemporary Jewish Museum, one of three American venues chosen to host the touring show.

"Our intent behind the show was to treat Sendak holistically: as an artist, as a craftsman, as a collector, as a reader, as a storyteller, and as a human being," explains exhibition curator Patrick Rodgers via e-mail. This proved challenging, given the sheer volume of Sendak's work. Rodgers had been poring over the more than 10,000 Sendak pieces that the Rosenbach holds, but didn't discover the secret until Sendak gave an interview in August 2007.

"[Sendak] said, 'You have to find something unique in each book, which perhaps even the author was not entirely aware of,'" Rodgers recalls. "'...That's what you hold onto, and that's what you add to the pictures: a whole Other Story, that you believe in, that you think is there.'" This concept guides viewers through the four major sections of the exhibition. "Kids: Innocence and

Experience" explores Sendak's visual and emotional portrayal of children's lives, while "Beasts of Burden" devotes itself to his fanciful creatures. "Influences: Family, Friends and Inspirations" details the personal experiences that inspire his work, and "Settings: Cityscapes, Landscapes, and Scenery" delves into the backstory behind Sendak's backgrounds.

Some Sendak books hint at an Other Story, such as the subtle visual allusions to Nazi concentration camps in his 1988 adaptation of Grimm's **Dear Mili**. Some Other Stories are explored more directly, such as the specter of homelessness in 1993's **We Are All in the Dumps with Jack and Guy**. Many Other Stories are personally significant to Sendak, which can complicate his collaborations with other authors. "...As much as [Sendak] believes in finding his own Other Story to tell in his illustrations, he also respects the authors he illustrates and tries to work with their vision," Rodgers affirms. The curator cites Sendak's illustrations in Isaac Bashevis Singer's book of Yiddish folktales as a perfect melding of the Other Story with the more obvious one. Sendak drew many of his fictionalized characters straight from family photographs taken in the Jewish enclaves of Poland. "So you read the book and you know it's folklore," Rodgers notes, "but what you're also seeing—the Other Story—is that Sendak's family populates that folklore, and that he merged the fantastical and the real."

Sendak's best-known blend of fantasy and reality is 1963's **Where The Wild Things Are**, the tale of a little boy's fantasized meeting with jungle monsters. The book went on to sell millions of copies in several languages, but was denounced by some critics (and child psychiatrist Bruno Bettelheim) as dangerous and frightening for children. (See pages 111-113 of John Cech's **Angels and Wild Things: The Archetypal Poetics of Maurice Sendak** [Pennsylvania State University Press, 1995] for an overview of complaints made against the book.) When

Sendak received a prestigious Caldecott Medal for the book in 1964, he acknowledged this tension in his acceptance speech. "Truthfulness to life—both fantasy life and factual life—is the basis of all great art," Sendak affirmed. "This is the beginning of my answer to the question: Where did you get such a crazy, scary idea for a book?" The young hero Max and his Wild Things have permanently captured the public's imagination, appearing in print commercials, posters for literacy campaigns, and even their own opera in the past 47 years. The controversy also has endured, rising and waning at different times. (For instance, a special session of the 1976 Children's Literature Association conference heatedly debated the book's "disturbing possibilities.") The 2009 live-action film adaptation of the book, directed by Spike Jonze from a script by Dave Eggers, has found critical as well as commercial success. Are current audiences more willing to acknowledge the uneasiness and ambiguity Sendak evokes?

"I honestly don't know if audiences today are more accepting of the difficult situations and insinuations present in Sendak's work," Rodgers says. "There have always been—and perhaps will always be—a segment of his readers and the general population who don't care much for the hard truths he puts forward (and even some who take offense to them)." Clearly, it is Sendak's honesty, always tempered by his love and concern for humanity, that has allowed his work to remain relevant for decades. Happily, the artist continues working to this day. Who knows what Maurice Sendak's next 80 years will bring?

POSTSCRIPT: Maurice Sendak remained an active and influential artist in his later years, publishing his final book, **Bumble-Ardy**, eight months before he died in May 2012. To learn more about him, his work, and the exhibition, visit the Rosenbach Museum's website at www.rosenbach.org.

SANTA CRUZ CHOCOLATE FESTIVAL
[Adapted from "Chocoholic Alert" in the Winter 2010 Student Guide]

If the word "chocolate" conjures up images of overly sweet, grainy Halloween candy, you are about to enter a whole new world. Chocolate is a worthy partner to sweet and savory flavors, used to enrobe everything from dried nectarines to hickory-smoked bacon. Fine chocolates boast increasingly exotic fillings featuring vintage wines, spice infusions, or even extra-virgin olive oil. Bittersweet, single-origin, and artisanal chocolates show off the subtle flavor nuances of chocolate itself. Perhaps you are more traditional, happiest with a comforting slab of dark, creamy fudge. Think of your favorite form of chocolate, and it's almost guaranteed that you can find a great example made right in Santa Cruz County. Each January, there is be one place where you can sample all of these and many more: the Santa Cruz Chocolate Festival.

The Chocolate Festival first came to life in mid-2007, when a group of UCSC-affiliated women were looking for fundraising ideas. One woman came from a town that hosted a very successful annual chocolate festival. The idea was broached to UCSC Women's Club board member Lorraine Margon, who had just been elected fundraising coordinator of the group. The first Chocolate Festival took place in February 2008 at what was then the Attic in downtown Santa Cruz. The event drew more than 600 people, and was deemed a roaring success. Not only has the festival become a yearly event, it is now held at the Boardwalk's Cocoanut Grove ballroom to accommodate more people. (Margon, who continues to chair the event, is happy about a new floor plan for this year's festival that will allow extra space for vendors and attendees alike.)

During the festival's brief existence, Margon already has seen several trends evolve. While it may be a given that "there are very, very few people who don't like chocolate," their tastes have become more sophisticated with each passing year. "People are enjoying a higher quality of chocolate," Margon notes, "and more and more fine chocolate businesses are springing up." One pioneer in artisanal chocolate is Santa Cruz's Richard Donnelly, who began creating and selling handmade chocolates in 1988. Though his wares have been honored by everyone from **Chocolatier** magazine to the EuroChocolate Festival in Perugia, Italy, Donnelly still produces his chocolates in a tiny shop on Mission Street. "Donnelly Chocolates has certainly put Santa Cruz on the map in the world of chocolate," Margon affirms. "You can travel to other fine chocolate establishments worldwide, and you can be sure that they know of Richard Donnelly and his chocolates." Margon singles out another local institution, one cherished since it first opened in 1915. "Marini's Candies has also gotten a lot of national recognition, especially from the Food Network, and they are also known for their Chocolate Covered Bacon. In addition, there are quite a number of local businesses who produce wonderful chocolate products right here." Several of these companies, such as Ashby Confections of Aptos and Scotts Valley's Chocolate Visions, will be vendors at the upcoming festival.

If you are one of those misguided souls who would call a chocolate festival an exercise in hedonism, rest assured that it will benefit a fine cause. The UCSC Women's Club created the event to fund scholarships for re-entry students. Margon explains, "Re-entry students are defined as undergraduates twenty-five years and older, graduate students twenty-nine and over, students who have had a substantial break in their formal education, military veterans, and all students who are also parents." Since they fall outside the traditional campus

61

demographic, these students do not always receive the academic and financial support that they need. The Women's Club has addressed this problem by awarding nearly 300 scholarships totaling $160,000 over the past 30 years. (Though its name suggests otherwise, anyone in the local campus community is welcome to join the Women's Club. Information about the organization, as well as links to resources for re-entry students, can be found at womensclub.ucsc.edu.)

Clearly, chocolate is much more than a simple treat. It brings happiness to young and old in the best and worst of times, and has become important to many people's quality of life. "Chocolate seems to be recession-resistant," Margon says, "as chocolate sales have not been deterred during the economic downturn." It makes sense, then, that the Santa Cruz Chocolate Festival has become the top Women's Club fundraiser, more than doubling the amount of money the group raises locally. Festivalgoers will get to savor some remarkable treats, while helping more at-risk students than ever before. There is no better reason to enjoy the irresistible power of chocolate.

POSTSCRIPT: The festival is entering its eighth year, and has raised more than $60,000 in scholarships as of this writing. Margon continues to work with the Women's Club and the festival, and was honored as Chocoholic of the Year at the 2013 event. For more information on the Chocolate Festival and the programs it benefits, visit http://womensclub.ucsc.edu/fundraising/chocolate-festival/.

SURF CITY SANTA CRUZ: A WAVE OF INSPIRATION
[From the Spring 2010 Student Guide]

On the surface, surfing is a straightforward interaction between one person and the ocean. Yet, this deceptively simple activity has imprinted itself on the hearts of generations of Santa Cruz County residents. The intense, temperamental relationship forged between local surfers and the coast has affected our leisure, our commerce, our local way of life. But how does it affect our artistic creativity? The Santa Cruz Museum of Art and History contacted a staggering array of local artists and artisans, all of whom are longtime surfers, to find the answer. The result is the current exhibition Surf City Santa Cruz: A Wave of Inspiration.

The museum's ground floor is devoted to the craft of surfing, displaying objects that unite form and function. Viewers can trace the evolution of surfboard and wetsuit design over the years, and notice where the artistic and the technical merge. This is especially important to surfboard shapers who create their work to order, since they have to consider the demands of their clients as well as those of the ocean. Gary Hughes, who has surfed for nearly fifty years and shaped boards for more than twenty, reflects on this complicated relationship.

"Surfing is so personal, and a board that is a dog for one person is perfect for another," Hughes notes. "I don't shape for pros, and the needs of average surfers are a compromise between performance, paddling, and predictability. One of the difficulties is that, once you make an exceptional board for a certain person's needs, he tends to want that, and is less open to the inevitable truth that, like other artists, shapers must progress through trial and error." While shaping machines can make differences from board to board more predictable, there will always be factors that make each board different. "The very best surfers can often tell the difference between subtle changes, but often do not understand the synergy that links the design features together." Hughes notices a shift among the demanding surfers of Santa Cruz County. "At this time, surfers are unusually open to designs that are not clones of what the pros are riding. Old boards, experimental boards, and new fin designs are proliferating."

When shapers are surfers themselves, this is bound to affect their design. Personal experiences, needs, and philosophies can be taken into account, leading to innovations that can help their clients as well. Take the legendary Johnny Rice, who has custom-shaped surfboards for more than fifty years. "We are in our seventies," Rosemari Reimers Rice explains, "so we have boards that float us high and paddle easily into the waves." The Rices' boards also reflect their concern for the environment through the use of a special UV solar resin. "The water is the Mother Earth's blood, and if it gets polluted, then she's going to get sick," Johnny Rice has said. "Then what's she going to do?" [See "The Good Life of Surfboard Shaper Johnny Rice" by Nina Wu, archived online at
http://www.coastnews.com/sports/surfboards/rice.htm.]

It is no coincidence that the Rices' firsthand experience with the ocean has heightened their social awareness. In his surf culture chronicle **Stoked!**, Drew Kampion explains that surfers tend to be at the forefront of environmental movements because they experience "such intimate contact with the natural world at a time when most humans are increasingly sealed off in artificial surroundings." So, through their commercial shaping work, the Rices are able to act on their beliefs in a way that helps surfers and nonsurfers alike.

The ground floor is rounded out by a display of surf logos and other commercial art. This prepares viewers for the paintings, ceramics, sculptures and other fine art objects to be seen on the second floor, but it also reminds them that the distinction between fine art and commercial art may not be as clear-cut as popular opinion may proclaim. Hughes makes a living as a fine artist and a commercial artist, and his unique situation highlights this ambiguity. "I do a little surf art, but do not, in any way, consider myself a surf artist," he affirms. "However, I am very much into doing artwork on surfboards, with airbrush and marking pens. Painting on surfboards is pretty fun."

The artists of the second floor often have one foot in both worlds as well. Vince Broglio is renowned for his glassing (that is, his work applying epoxies and finishes to shaped surfboards). He has run his glassworks shop since 1990, but a chance event caused him to view his glassing in a whole new way. "It boiled down to when [famous glasser Gordon] 'Grubby' Clark closed his factory in 2005, and a light bulb went off," Broglio reveals. "I looked at my room and my [equipment] rack and said, 'Wow, that kind of looks like art with all the colors, fiberglass, and ink all over.'" Thus inspired, Broglio experimented with sculpture using his glassing equipment, while his main career continued to flourish. Broglio's work is presented in the fine art section of the exhibition, but he downplays the artist label. "I have no art background at all...People who come into my shop go 'Wow, you know, that's artwork.' I never really thought about it like that."

As many surf objects are not necessarily created as artwork, much of the second floor's artwork at first seems unrelated to surfing. Some of the exhibition's artists prefer to keep their two loves separate, using surfing as a source of relaxation that is unrelated to their work. "I cannot say that surfing influences my work," fine artist David Kimball Anderson affirms. "Surfing is a separate activity for me...Many times I will pass up a swell because I would rather work in my studio."

Other artists enjoy an ever-changing relationship between surfing and their muse. Marvin Plummer's earliest works depicted waves, but currently the artist is known for his portraits of dogs and Depression-era subjects. Even though Plummer has become more specialized, surfing remains an important source of mental respite and creativity for him. "I'd say that surfing and our area here in Santa Cruz are tremendous influences on my work," he says. "A good day of surfing resets the mind and really helps me to focus in the studio...Surfing affects all aspects of my life for the better, but most certainly my art." Recently, Plummer has returned to surfing as a subject, completing a surf mural of Steamer Lane on display at 820 Swift Street. "The mural project and this **Surf City Santa Cruz** exhibition have really stoked me to make more 'surf art.'"

The third floor is devoted to the most dramatic example of "surf art": the genre of surf photography. While the images convey the beauty and excitement of a day on the waves, the process presents its own set of challenges. Internationally acclaimed surf photographer Nikki Brooks embraces this unpredictability. "Things never look the same with the naked eye as they do through the lens. Perspective is how one chooses to look through the lens, how far down the beach, the height of the tripod, the speed of the shutter, foreground and background," she explains. "When you have all those factors dialed in, the results can be interesting and different than how a beach-goer may see the same surfer riding the same wave."

Brooks sees her surfing as a great influence on her artistic process. "I like to take photos from a surfer's point of view," she says. "From the water this happens most often, since it is the view a surfer sees from the lineup. Being a surfer helps me photograph surfers, since I understand the dynamics of the waves and how surfers ride them. Other stuff is cool too, like watching how the surfer I am shooting rides a wave and the lines he / she draws, and anticipating what they might do next." This empathy with the surfer in the water not only leads to superior photographs, it has an unexpected side benefit: "I think it helps me become a better surfer since I watch surfing so much," Brooks relates, "and it is of course super-rewarding when I am surfing and not shooting!"

The nonsurfer, for better or worse, often has a stereotypical image of a surfer in mind when the subject comes up. Even a cursory glance at the exhibition's list of artists will kill this myth once and for all. What fascinates is the wide range of difference among these artists as individuals. For instance, local chef Jim Denevan may or may not have anything else in common with San Jose State professor Stan Welsh, yet both love surfing and use it to inspire very different forms of artwork. Likewise, any two surfers may share no common interests except their affection for the water. Why does surfing appeal to so many different personalities?

Vince Broglio has a theory. "Lots of us probably got into it at an early age. I first learned to surf when I was 11, and knew I wanted to build boards and all that, but I think a lot of people just love it who are professionals." He notes that firefighters and police officers often have downtime that allows for surfing, and implies that people in high-stress jobs probably welcome the opportunity to clear their minds through a day on the water. "I think a lot of professionals started out surfing when they were kids. So, it's always been in their blood, and...it's hard to let go once you've gotten into it." In other words, you don't think about becoming a surfer when you grow up; you grow up a surfer, and let surfing shape the person you become. Thanks to this exhibition, now everyone can see how surfing has shaped a city of individuals into Surf City, Santa Cruz.

"SOMETHIN'S HAPPENING HERE": THE BEAT OF THE BAY
[From the Spring 2010 Student Guide]

In 1963, San Francisco had one professional recording facility; by 1970, it had ten. In 1969, renowned music critic Ralph J. Gleason proclaimed, "San Francisco IS the Liverpool of America now." Yet, the Bay Area's musical explosion was not inspired by the British Invasion, nor was it limited to the 49 square miles of San Francisco. Those looking for the full picture should seek out **Somethin's Happening Here: Bay Area Rock 'n' Roll 1963-1973**, currently on display at San Francisco's Museum of Performance and Design.

Note the emphasis on "Bay Area rock," as opposed to "San Francisco rock." Visitors expecting an insular scene spanning the intersection of Haight-Ashbury will be fascinated to discover the diverse sounds that flourished in San Jose, Sacramento, and our own Santa Cruz, to name but a few places. While the likes of Grace Slick and Carlos Santana receive their usual exposure, the exhibition champions musicians such as We Five lead singer Beverly Bivens and Flamin' Groovies mastermind Roy Loney, not household names but influential in their own right. "There are indeed still misconceptions to fight," notes co-curator and music historian Alec Palao, "in the same way that so many critics, historians and commentators still believe the whole scene was half a dozen bands and a bunch of also-rans."

The show's many music and video clips illustrate the problem: namely, the huge variety of music that emerged from the Bay Area during the era. As Ben Fong-Torres muses in an essay written for Rhino Records' Palao-produced **Love Is The Song We Sing** compilation boxed set, it's difficult to "make obvious musical connections between [Big Brother and the Holding Company's] raw blues, [Jefferson Airplane's] folk-rock, and [Country Joe & the Fish's] acid visions." Factor in Bay Area garage-rock, soul, jazz, country, Latin, and avant-garde acts, and the idea of a definable "San Francisco Sound" is quickly exposed as myth.

Once geographic and genre limitations were punctured, how would the curators accurately portray the phenomenon? "We created a target list of musicians and bands we hoped to cover," co-curator Melissa Leventon explains, "and organized the exhibition by sections: Venues, Events, Recording, Advertising and Promotion, and Style. So that directed our searching, and we were aiming for broad rather than in-depth representation." As she and Palao sifted through the era's artifacts, most key objects emerged from the years 1965 through 1970. These include everything from a fringed vest belonging to Sly Stone to vintage light show equipment, not to mention many concert posters from venues throughout the Bay Area.

When asked about favorite items in the show, Palao points to the inclusion of Jerry Garcia's Captain Trips hat as "a real coup," given its place in early San Francisco rock iconography. Leventon, for her part, is amazed by the imposing three-dimensional Bill Walker painting used as the album cover for the Grateful Dead's second album, **Anthem of the Sun**: "It's in a private collection in San Francisco and has never been displayed before."

But make no mistake, the show soars highest when it reveals the secret heroes of Bay Area music. Palao is particularly proud of the photos depicting the lesser-known bands, including the Creedence Clearwater Revival precursor Golliwogs: "You likely wouldn't see those in other, more mainstream exhibitions." Leventon fervently hopes that the show conveys "the understanding that there was a lot more going on here than just the Grateful Dead and the Jefferson Airplane." The museum is located at 893B Folsom Street in San Francisco; contact (415) 255-4800 or www.mpdsf.org for more information.

ART ON THE EDGE

[The following version is expanded from the original that appeared in the Fall 2010 Student Guide]

Santa Cruz has been a musical hotbed over the years, gaining notoriety for its thriving folk, punk, and reggae scenes. When most music fans associate a certain genre with the city, "hip-hop" is not likely to spring to mind. This might change once they read the graphic novel series **Nineteen Eighty Five**, created by Santa Cruz native James Reitano. The semi-autobiographical story centers on fifteen-year-old graffiti artist Count, his friends, and their adventures in the local hip-hop community.

What made 1985 such a watershed year for Reitano? "For myself, hip-hop and graffiti were something, I think, that gave me my first real identity," he noted via e-mail. "I was part of this movement, and, by 1985, it seemed like it was in full swing, although by the end of the year, things were starting to peter out a bit." The artist revealed his own theory regarding the unheralded nature of Santa Cruz's hip-hop culture: "Santa Cruz [hip-hop] has never really been documented too much, probably because it always seemed so hard to get anything done there. The irony is, I had to move OUT of Santa Cruz to write a comic about it."

In the twenty-five years since the events of the comic, graffiti artists such as Fafi and the late Jean-Michel Basquiat have crossed over to gain acceptance and success in the art world. Even so, the graffiti-themed plotline of **Nineteen Eighty Five** evokes strong feelings in some people. In her online review of the series, Johanna Draper Carlson decried Count as "a vandal teen," complaining, "Even when he gets caught, it's an excuse for him (and the author?) to justify his actions as an art...I just felt bad for everyone whose property he was defacing." [See

71

Comics Worth Reading blog, June 13, 2010. The quote is archived at comicsworthreading.com/2010/06/13/slush-pile-charlatan-deformitory-fchs-ouija-interviews-more/]

Since Count is inspired in part by the young Reitano, did the artist worry about making him sympathetic, or alienating people close to him with the story? Reitano pointed out, "I think with any sort of autobiographical work, you have to bend things. Events that might have been weeks apart happen on the same night, etc." He added, "No one's seemed too bothered by it yet, we'll see. Most folks I knew from back then seem thrilled about it thus far."

On the other hand, accurately conveying the music and mood involved was a real concern, since music and comics are so different from each other. "For the comic, the music is really in the background, and it's basically the story and the characters running the show," Reitano affirmed. The artist devised the ingenious solution of including an exclusive, specially-curated mix CD with each volume of the series. "With the soundtracks for the book, I was going to do them myself," Reitano explained. "My friend Peanut Butter Wolf asked me, 'How come you didn't ask me to do a mix?,' and I took that as an offer. He did the first one, and Kutmasta Kurt offered up his mix for part two (which was incredible, it even uses parts of his old KUSP radio show)!" Reitano stressed authenticity for the CDs as well as his comics, noting "I'd like them to be by people who were around back then."

Reitano has combined his love of music and drawing throughout his career. Besides his commercial art work for the likes of the Wu-Tang Clan, he has directed and animated music videos for everyone from Kool Keith to pop-punk legends The Dickies. For Reitano, the evolution was natural. "I'd taken a few classes out of interest, and messed around a bit. I got asked to make a music video (that I worked insanely hard on), and it seemed to get a good reception, with other folks asking for them. Next thing I knew, I was an animator." Several factors allowed the artist to become comfortable working in more than one medium. "Moving to L.A. opened all sorts of doors to me, and, it was amazing how responsive clients were, and how serious minded people are here about the work. Plus, software was developed which enabled novices like myself to create these things I'd always dreamt of. My animations have always been design / illustration emphasized, so comics aren't too far of a stretch...I've been drawing comics since I was a little kid."

As a former Santa Cruz resident who now lives in Los Angeles, Reitano reflected briefly on the cities. "L.A.'s an industry town, with all of the baggage connected to that, but with the positive sides I noted above. Nor-Cal is much more soulful but maybe a bit more angry. I don't know." He considers the long-hyped Northern / Southern California rivalry to be a nonissue. "Most folks down here don't seem to care too much. Nor-Cal people hate L.A. the same way most of the world does. But like everywhere else, it's not the city, it's people who change when they get here. I've seen it happen dozens of times. [It's] kind of like when someone goes to Vegas and acts like a goofball. It's not Vegas's fault."

While Reitano has several projects in the discussion stage, he is focused on completing **Nineteen Eighty Five**. "I've had these books planned for about four years and finally got a chance to do it," Reitano said. "I think if you have that project you've always wanted to do but were putting off, just do it now, don't postpone it anymore. It's never going to be perfect, and it'll definitely get stale while you're working on it, but you can't let that stop you from completing a passion project."

AUTHOR'S NOTE: As of this 2014 update, six volumes of the series are now available. Visit nineteen85.com to see samples of the graphic novel, or to buy your own copy. To see clips of Reitano's video work and read the TFU Studios blog, go to tfustudios.com.

SFMOMA: THE ANNIVERSARY SHOW
[From the Fall 2010 Student Guide]

Over its 75 years, the San Francisco Museum of Modern Art has influenced art and culture worldwide, not just in northern California. From Jackson Pollock's paintings to William Eggleston's photographs, from Eva Hesse's sculptures to Matthew Barney's multimedia installations, the museum's exhibitions have not only reflected their cultural landscape, but shaped it. Through January 16, 2011, museum visitors can experience this impact in **The Anniversary Show**.

How can 75 years be condensed accurately into one exhibition? Sarah Roberts, who curated the show with Janet Bishop and Corey Keller, talked about the project's evolution via e-mail. "We were asked by our Director, Neal Benezra, to organize an exhibition in honor of the museum's 75th Anniversary. The subject matter was entirely up to us, and we decided to focus on the moments when the museum has been particularly forward-looking, or moved the conversation about contemporary art forward in a significant way. In other words, we chose to highlight moments when the history of the museum has intersected with the history of art in some meaningful fashion."The curators did not approach the task with a specific agenda. "Once we settled on the above thesis, we began to discuss the possible 'moments' we wished to highlight. The checklist evolved very organically as we narrowed our choices. We decided that each and every object had to have a story behind it, a direct connection to the story being told in each gallery." The vast holdings were winnowed to roughly 400 items. "There were some artworks that were clearly important to our history, among them very recognizable works such as Frida Kahlo's **Frida and Diego Rivera** (1931) and Jeff Koons's **Michael Jackson and Bubbles** (1988). During the research phase, we were thrilled to rediscover other less well-known, very strong artworks, such as the sculptures by Robert Howard and Adaline Kent, that also represent significant moments in the history of California art."

The museum's holdings have differed wildly in their styles and artistic media throughout the years. To reflect them all properly, the curators had to sidestep the usual approach of highlighting a particular artist or movement. Instead, they concentrated on a cast of characters no less important to the museum's daily workings: donors and officials who directly affected the museum's acquisitions. "The opportunity to represent the museum's history as a collection of voices, as the combined effort of a range of impassioned individuals, was the most gratifying aspect of organizing this exhibition," Roberts noted. "So often museums come across as depersonalized institutions, but in every case, the artworks in museum collections come in through the passion or generosity of someone who made a choice to give or purchase that artwork. Those choices and those individuals make up who we are as a museum, and they knit us into the social fabric of the Bay Area."

This daring approach presented potential hazards. These unfamiliar names, as well as the acquisitions process, would need explanation in a way that would not turn off the casual visitor. "The main challenge with looking at individuals was to keep the show from feeling too insular," Roberts explained. "We worked very hard to create a balance of looking inward and outward, backward and forward."

An unsung hero emerged. Grace McCann Morley (1900-1985) served as the museum's founding director from 1935 to 1958, and the exhibition shows her deep imprint. "She almost single-handedly established an audience for modern art on the West coast in the 1930s and 1940s," Roberts revealed. "Morley mounted more than 100 exhibitions a year on a shoestring budget through sheer force of will and dedication to the cause of enriching people's lives through art." The director had to contend with disapproving skeptics as well. An anonymous letter in March 1935 chastised Morley: "Maybe you should see an oculist to be pleased with a picture so unfair to God's creation of human beings with healthy eyes." The offending painting was **Merely Hit**, by the now-beloved Paul Klee.

Changing times and world events influenced and often complicated Morley's work. When the museum mounted the first U.S. exhibition by Argentine painter Emilio Pettoruti in 1942, Morley personally defended the artist against allegations that he was a Fascist. She arranged to have Picasso's **Guernica** displayed in 1939, before the United States entered World War II. During the war, the museum piloted the Red Cross's Arts and Skills program, which rehabilitated wounded veterans through upper-level arts and crafts instruction. Morley's only obligation was to art and artists, yet she worked for the greater good. It's no wonder that Roberts called her "a force of nature about whom too little has been written."

The exhibition's post-Morley sections indicate transitions in the art world as well as the museum. The San Francisco Art Association annual shows, running between 1959 and 1966, featured new artists alongside established ones, figurative work alongside abstraction. Highlights from specific exhibitions demonstrate the dizzying array of philosophies and approaches that embody modern art, featuring everything from the museum's influential Pop Art holdings to wooden chairs and everyday (if well-designed) household objects.

Roberts was unable to single out a single favorite in the show, citing works by Barry McGee, Adaline Kent, and Felix Gonzalez-Torres while adding, "I could easily list ten more." To make sense of the exhaustive selection, the curator highly recommends the free multimedia handheld tour available in the museum atrium. "It features interviews with artists, curators, and scholars, as well as video footage, poems, and music, all of which are accessed on demand so that each visitor can tailor their own experience of the exhibition." This interactive aspect may well indicate future directions for modern artists as well as museumgoers. Whatever happens in the art world's next 75 years and beyond, may the San Francisco Museum of Modern Art continue to be at its forefront.

The museum is located at 151 Third Street (between Mission and Howard), San Francisco. For museum hours and admission fees, visit www.sfmoma.org or phone (415) 357-4000.

RETRO-TECH: BACK TO THE FUTURE
[From the Winter 2011 Student Guide]

In today's world, it's become nearly impossible to keep pace with advances in technology.

Clock radios and calculators, so useful fifty or even thirty years ago, are now all but obsolete. Go back even further, and the differences are more dramatic. It's hard to fathom that the schooner, for instance, was as vital to 19th-century communication and commerce as the airplane is to ours.

These technological specimens of the past may be quaint curiosities to most, but a diverse group of artists has transformed them into thought-provoking multimedia works. Witness **Retro-Tech**, on display now at the San Jose Museum of Art.

How did discarded technology find its true potential in the heart of Silicon Valley? The spark came from the museum's involvement with San Jose's 2010 Zero One Biennial, a collaborative fusion of the artistic and the technical in presentations throughout the city's museums and public sites. "This year's theme was 'Build Your Own World,' so that theme was about how artists can develop kinds of solutions and ideas that address some of the challenges of the 21st century, how artists can envision a new world," explained Kristen Evangelista, the exhibition's curator. "So with that in mind, I decided to focus on how artists were approaching technology; looking at obsolete technology or technology of the past, you might say, almost in a nostalgic way, but showing a kind of reluctance to the latest, hippest, newest gadget and instead mining things that have been explored in the past, and seeing if techniques or materials from the past had potential that has yet been untapped or to be reconfigured."

Several works bring this potential to dramatic life in the exhibition. In her **Vintage Packaging For Animation** (2009), the French artist Katya Bonnenfant refurbished mid-20th century calculators and clock radios, merging them with iPods to display fanciful animations. The numerals on the clocks morph into tiny, dynamic beings who move in unpredictable ways. It is as if the objects have spirits inside that are waiting to be rediscovered.

Other artists make the virtual world physically tangible. Take Victoria Scott and Scott Kildall's **Gift Horse** (2010), specially commissioned for this exhibition. The artists designed a Trojan horse for digital existence in the virtual Second Life community, then fashioned an imposing three-dimensional version from recycled paperboard. They then conducted workshops where visitors learned to craft paper sculptures, which were placed inside the horse. When the horse was installed in the museum, a trap door was opened that released the public artwork into the museum space. (Patrons are welcome to add new paper crafts during the exhibition's run.) The work powerfully combines ancient mythology and modern imagination, complex calculations and exacting handiwork. While Evangelista does not consider this work to represent the entire exhibition's ideals, she finds **Gift Horse**'s contradictions to be a useful discussion point. "I think part of how I see that project that they did is that there's a strain that goes through the exhibition about the intersection of low and high technology, things that are really simple and things that are really advanced...one aspect of their project is rooted in Second Life and the virtual world, it's very cutting-edge, but then the objects that they try to bring to life in the physical space are very simply made, like humble materials and this very painstaking Japanese paper-folding tradition."

Our culture has a schizophrenic relationship with technology. Media outlets are quick to hype the latest devices, while decrying the impersonality they bring to our lives. It can be easy to feel that as technology becomes more pervasive, it takes away human autonomy. In contrast, the objects of **Retro-Tech** bear the stamp of human imagination, and are clearly at the control of fertile, artistic minds. Was this positive view of technology intentional?

"That's an interesting question, because that wasn't really something I considered when I was putting the show together: how does this reflect humans' relationship with technology," Evangelista revealed. "In retrospect, the work is very lighthearted, and the artists are very much in control of technology; they're using it as a tool to solve problems that they've identified. So, I think maybe it was coincidental that the show ended up taking that approach to technology, but I think that the artists do see technology as something that's positive, that it has potential."

The exhibition can lead the viewer to reconsider the definition of technology itself. The featured short film **There's More Than One Way To Skin A Sheep**, made in 2007 by Jennifer Allora and Guillermo Calzadilla, depicts a bicyclist in bustling downtown Istanbul. He blows into a tulum, an ancient form of Turkish bagpipe made from a sheep's carcass, in order to inflate his punctured tire. The musical notes disrupt the urban landscape, affecting passersby in a way that more complicated objects do not.

"Is a piece of paper and a pencil, writing on a piece of paper, a form of technology? I think the works of the exhibition definitely raise that question of, is technology just about having tools to do everyday things in our lives? I think that's sort of the approach that the exhibition takes, really opens the definition of technology," Evangelista replied. "That was really intentional on my part, because in the past, exhibitions we've had at the museum in conjunction with Zero One have been very much focused on the cutting-edge technology...I really wanted to do something different that was more open, and also more accessible to people, to really rethink how technology is part of their daily lives."

What makes an object a technological marvel: its novelty, its usefulness? **Retro-Tech** adds an overlooked but important criterion: the ability to stoke the imagination.

The San Jose Museum of Art is located at 110 South Market Street in San Jose, and is open Tuesday through Sunday, 11 a.m. to 5 p.m. For more information, phone (408) 271-6840 or visit www.sjmusart.org. For links to the artists, visit the Zero One Biennial site at 01sj.org/2010/exhibitions/retro-tech.

ALEX EYLAR: CONQUERING TINSELTOWN BRICK BY BRICK
[From the Winter 2012 Student Guide]

After Alex Eylar graduated from UCSC's Film and Digital Media department, he moved to Southern California to make a name for himself in the film industry. In his rising career, the young auteur has paid homage to all the greats: Akira Kurosawa, Alfred Hitchcock, Ole Kirk Christiansen. If that last name is unfamiliar to you, it's because it does not come from the world of cinema at all. Christiansen is the Danish carpenter who invented Lego building blocks in the 1930s. Eylar is best known for his startlingly detailed depictions of films as diverse as **The Shining** and The **King's Speech**, as well as his own elaborate scenarios, constructed through the medium of Legos.

Some might surmise that complex scenes rendered through children's toys is a madcap, Santa Cruz sort of idea. Actually, the Oakland native began his cinematic Lego experimentations even before he attended UCSC, pulling out his childhood collection of bricks in high school to create his first projects. Even so, Eylar acknowledged that UCSC provided subtle but pervasive influences on his cinematic evolution. "UCSC's approach to cinema is unique in that it's so specific and broad at the same time; it covers all the bases," he stated. "You can take something as general as World Cinema, or a course whose focus is as narrow as the films of Wong Kar-Wai or sexuality in cinema. It opens you up to areas of cinema you couldn't access before, and when you're trying to write movies—like I am—the more movies you know, the better."

Eylar's Lego scenes have drawn raves from the likes of **The New York Times** and London's **Daily Telegraph**, as well as notoriety throughout the Internet. Does he worry that all this attention will eventually overshadow his more traditional, "serious" projects? "I don't think the Lego scenes will detract from my credibility too much," he replied. "It's Lego; it's as innocent as they come. I haven't yet met someone who didn't think fondly of the stuff, or enjoy the scenes I build. Some people question my devotion to what they call a children's toy, but it's like any hobby: there are bound to be those that don't click with it."

During his UCSC career, Eylar found another creative outlet, one that was something of a happy accident. "I'd usually arrive 30 minutes early for class due to parking issues, and would basically kill time in the computer lab of the film building," he revealed. "I'd seen all sorts of minimalist movie posters online, and figured I'd try my hand. That's the origin story: they came out of boredom." With their stark and clever imagery, the artist's fifty-one posters (at the time of this writing) have earned kudos from the likes of the online trendspotting newsletter **Thrillist**, and are available for sale via the Imagekind webstore.

While the finished products may seem deceptively straightforward at first glance, the execution is often challenging. Eylar is particularly proud of his Lego version of **Inception**: "It required a full hallway, able to be turned-upside down for the appropriate shot. Not an easy build, but the final product is instantly recognizable, and that's the best you can hope for with these projects."

Likewise, Eylar's posters are not simple rehashes of familiar images, as he explained when discussing his favorite, depicting Kurosawa's **Rashomon**. "The challenge in making those posters is incorporating an idea; not just including one object and putting the title beneath it," he explained. "I think—I hope—the **Rashomon** poster pulled off a concise illustration of that movie's theme; that's why I like it."

Eylar currently pursues a Master of Fine Arts in screenwriting at Chapman University in Orange County. At the time of the interview, his short script, **Thunderboned**, had just been shot as a student film. Somehow, he still finds time to devise new posters and Lego scenes, which he continues to post online to the delight of fans everywhere. Even he can't predict what he'll do next, but one thing is certain: Alex Eylar may often work in miniature, but the scope of his imagination is large indeed.

To view or purchase Eylar's art prints and movie posters, visit aeylar.imagekind.com. His Lego scenes appear on his Flickr page, www.flickr.com/photos/hoyvinmayvin/.

BANDEMONIUM!
[From the Spring 2012 Student Guide]

THE ATOMIC ACES

In November 2009, Formaldebrides lead guitarist "Miss Mercy" Vaisseur began looking for a project to fill the "artistic void" following that band's breakup. Rhythm guitarist Chris Curtiss enlisted first. While cutting her former schoolmate Andrew's hair, Vaisseur asked the sometime musician if he could play upright bass. He replied, "No, but I'd like to try," and soon became known as Kung Fu. The bassist brought in Dr. Dave on lead guitar. Dave's friend Oliver Northrup had only played percussion in a marching band, but soon bashed the drums eagerly. All the elements of a supergroup were now in place, rising phoenix-like to become Santa Cruz's very own Atomic Aces.

The Aces' sound reflects its members' varied backgrounds, breaking genre bounds. As the band grew more comfortable playing together, it became easier to take risks. Northrup said, "We started mixing more styles in. More punk. Country, and so on." Songs are arranged collaboratively, adding cohesion to the different elements. Most original songs have been Vaisseur's thus far, but this is not a requirement. Curtiss wrote the melody for Aces standard "No Way Out,"and the story of Kung Fu's chorus for "I'll Chop Your Head Off" further illustrates the band's alchemy.

"It came to him in a dream," Vaisseur recounted. "When he played it and sang it for us, the verses miraculously appeared in one practice along with the melody for the rest of the song. It was like it was just meant to be."

The Aces began recording at Santa Cruz's Compound, run by Fury 66's Joe Clements. (Clements did some mastering work on the album, which Vaisseur considered a "very exciting" honor.) The project proceeded in fits and starts, where the band would pool money earned from live shows and then record a song or two at a time when resources permitted. Translating the Aces' intense live presence to record also proved challenging. The band repeatedly mentioned the extra precision and concentration involved, with Vaisseur taking pains to emphasize "the emotion of the lyrics, and what [I was] trying to portray with the story behind the song." Happily, **Bettie's Rage** was released in September 2011, to the delight of the band as well as fans. "The final result is that you get to finally hear yourself through the ears of the audience, because it sounds completely different when you're listening than when you're playing," Vaisseur enthused. "That's what's really rewarding for me." The album is available at Streetlight Records, and online from iTunes, CDBaby, and Amazon.

The Atomic Aces have shot two professional music videos, which can be seen on the band's YouTube channel. You can book the Atomic Aces through their Facebook page, or get in touch the old-fashioned way by calling (831) 234-5341.

JACKIE ROCKS

In just over six years, Jackie Rocks has racked up a list of accomplishments that would put most veteran bands to shame. The band has played more than 400 shows, including the prestigious National Association of Music Merchants (NAMM) industry convention in winter 2011. The Santa Cruz group has won local and national awards, is sponsored by Daisy Rock Guitars, and performs frequently at San Francisco 49ers games and events at Candlestick Park.

Have I mentioned that Jackie Rocks' oldest member is just nineteen?

For 17-year-old singer-songwriter-guitarist Jacklyn Partida, there is no secret to the band's success. "Our bass player

De'Andre [Warren] and I have managed to keep the band going with different members coming in and out, but we always make sure we keep practicing and playing shows." She pointed to the addition of drummer Greg Brock three years ago as something that really cemented the band's identity. When asked how Jackie Rocks has evolved, Partida explained, "Our sound has gotten heavier over the past few years, making it hard rock with punk and metal overtones...yet it is also very melodic and has a lot of vocal harmonies." The harmonies are key to the band's crossover appeal, making it "easy for all ages to enjoy the music," even those who usually prefer other genres: "[They] end up appreciating what we do."

While Jackie Rocks embodies the term "hard-rocking power trio" proudly, the band's musical palette doesn't end with guitar, bass, and drums. Partida is an accomplished clarinet and piano player as well. Self-taught bassist Warren plays the saxophone and French horn, and Partida noted that "he can play just about any wind instrument" if a song calls for it. The band is living proof of the value of musical education in public schools, and Partida reflected on the effect of classical training on the band's decidedly modern arrangements and songwriting. "It has helped us to learn our instruments better and become better musicians overall," she noted, adding that the members continue to be very involved in their school music programs. "For De'Andre and me, it all started back at Shoreline Middle School in band class."

Jackie Rocks released a self-titled CD in 2006, and has appeared on several compilations. The band is gearing up for several high-profile shows, including a slot in the Girls Rock national tour beginning in Los Angeles this spring. In July, Partida will perform guitar at the Cabrillo Festival's Hidden World of Girls event, working with four other female composers sponsored by National Public Radio. To kick things off, Jackie Rocks will play the Young Artists Showcase at the Rio Theatre on April 21st. For song clips and booking information, visit www.jackierocksofficial.com.

POSTSCRIPT: The Atomic Aces finished recording a new EP, **My Kind of Devil**, in June 2014. Jackie Partida began attending the Berklee College of Music in Boston in 2012, while bassist De'Andre Warren started at the University of Chicago that year. While Jackie Rocks appears to be on hiatus, Partida's musical career is busier than ever. As of September 2014, her bands include the indie-pop project Dressed in Roses, and the goth-metal act Beautiful Deception. She is also lead guitarist for the Stellar Corpses, singer-guitarist in Requiem, and guitarist / backup vocalist for the Black Tigers. Visit www.facebook.com/jackierocksband for the latest information.

YOUR ENDLESS SUMMER OF ART
[Originally printed in Summer Santa Cruz 2012]

Santa Cruz County residents have always known that they lived in an artist's paradise. In November 2011, **The Atlantic** confirmed this impression, surprising the rest of the country. Using methodology dubbed "the location quotient," **The Atlantic** determined that the Santa Cruz area boasts nearly two and a half times the national average number of artists per capita. This placed our locale fifth on its top ten list, bested only by (in ascending order) Los Angeles, New York, San Francisco, and Santa Fe, New Mexico. The aesthetic bounty sometimes overwhelms newcomers to the local scene. Never fear. Here is your primer to the art world of Santa Cruz and its neighboring cities.

AROUND THE COUNTY

Since art flourishes everywhere you go in Santa Cruz County, it's appropriate that two beloved events spread through the entire area. For three whirlwind weekends in October, curious patrons can follow self-guided tours of professional artists' studios as part of Open Studios. The competitive application process means that the artists vary from year to year, but the end result is always an exhaustive showcase of fine art and craft. The first two weekends of October are split between North and South County (each going first on alternate years), with the third weekend usually devoted to a countywide encore. Contact the Cultural Council of Santa Cruz County for more information at ccscc.org, or phone (831) 475-9600.

If you can't wait for October, the First Friday Art Tour will sate your artistic wanderlust on a monthly basis, year-round. Sponsored by the Santa Cruz Institute of Contemporary Arts in a partnership with local arts venues, it allows you to explore artistic spaces around the county on the first Friday of each month. Traditional museums and galleries abound, but there is plenty of art to be found at participating shops and restaurants as well. Be sure to grab a copy of the monthly First Friday brochure for full details on that month's offerings. For more information, check out www.firstfridaysantacruz.com.

SANTA CRUZ

The grande dame of local arts institutions, the Santa Cruz Museum of Art and History has been revitalized under the direction of Nina Simon. The MAH has expanded its educational outreach and social engagement with visitors, and has added an interactive component to many of its exhibitions. Once you've explored the three floors of fine art and local historical artifacts, step onto the rooftop patio of the Mary and Harry Blanchard Sculpture Garden to enjoy a panoramic view of Santa Cruz. The museum is a mainstay of the First Friday Art Tour, and offers a free Third Friday event of its own (both with extended museum hours). Closed on Mondays, the museum is located at 705 Front Street in downtown Santa Cruz. Phone (831) 429-1964, or visit www.santacruzmah.org for more details.

If you're heading to or from the Boardwalk, take a brief detour off Ocean Street to the Santa Cruz Art League. Founded in 1919, the organization presents an average of fourteen art shows a year, including juried exhibitions. Classes and workshops are offered, and membership is open to anyone. The Art League, located at 526 Broadway in Santa Cruz, also boasts a theatrical space that hosts several performing groups on a rotating basis. The museum is open afternoons from Wednesday through Sunday. Dive in at www.scal.org, or phone (831) 426-5787.

SOUTH COUNTY

As this native eagerly points out, the nearby city of Watsonville received equal billing with Santa Cruz on **The Atlantic**'s list. Exhibitions here overflow their generally compact accommodations with a distinctive sense of place. From Thursday through Sunday (hours vary), the Pajaro Valley Gallery presents rotating exhibitions that emphasize local artists and cultural diversity. Since this small space could never contain all the talent involved, several satellite locations come into play. For instance, do not miss the annual **Sculpture IS** show at the Sierra Azul Nursery and Garden, on the outskirts of town off Highway 152. Every day from 9 a.m. to 5:30 p.m., June through October, visitors can marvel as breathtaking outdoor sculptures complement an impressive array of native plants.

The Pajaro Valley Gallery is located at 37 Sudden Street in downtown Watsonville, while the Sierra Azul Nursery and Garden is found at 2660 East Lake Avenue. Contact the Pajaro Valley Arts Council at (831) 722-3062 or www.pvarts.org for information about both venues.

NORTH COUNTY

Head north of Santa Cruz to Davenport, where Lundberg Studios has flourished since 1970. A staggering array of glass objects, from lamp shades to vases, are produced in an iridescent Art Nouveau style. Every piece of glass is formulated and hand-blown on site, which makes Lundberg Studios a rarity in the industry. A signature piece is the **Worldweight**, an opalescent paperweight created by the late founder Jim Lundberg, which depicts the globe in dazzling detail. Glassblowing demonstrations are given twice a year, but visitors are welcome at the studios at 131 Old Coast Road daily from 11 a.m. to 4 p.m. Call toll-free at (888) 423-9711 for information, or visit www.lundbergstudios.com

Afterward, a short trip northeast will bring you to the Santa Cruz Mountains Art Center, at 9341 Mill Street in Ben Lomond. The gallery displays a full range of local art, from paintings to ceramics, glass to textiles. Classes and lectures round out the nonprofit organization's offerings. Open Wednesday through Sunday from noon to 6 p.m. Phone (831) 336-3513 or visit www.mountainartcenter.org for more information.

There is not enough room to list the county's seemingly countless smaller galleries, not to mention the art to be found in its nontraditional venues. Take heart: if you devote a little time and curiosity to the search, hidden gems are sure to find you. What are you waiting for? It's time to begin your artistic pursuit, right here in Santa Cruz County!

THE MANY SIDES OF BEN SAMUEL
[Adapted from the Winter 2013 Student Guide]

How many computer scientists not only nab a starring role in a buzzworthy television series, but are proclaimed "the best reason to watch" the show by **The New York Times**? For that matter, how many working actors have helped to devise a groundbreaking computer game? Meet UCSC Ph.D student Ben Samuel, star of Hulu's series **Battleground** and co-creator of the social simulation game **Prom Week**.

Samuel was "pretty confident" that he wanted to pursue computer science and theatre arts majors as a UCSC undergrad, and holds bachelor's degrees in both fields of study. "I'm not sure if I can say that I'm more passionate about one field over the other—I find that I tend to be most excited about whatever I happen to be immersed in during any given day!" While the two disciplines seem completely different, Samuel explained their synergy. "The two fields definitely complement each other more than one might assume: as technical a discipline as computer science might be, developing software involves a lot of problem solving that requires a lot of the creativity, and even artistic expression, that is nurtured in a theatre program." Samuel credited computer science with "grounding" his work. "Theatre is such a subjective art, it was nice to be able to simultaneously work on projects that could be quantified as objectively correct. Either the program compiles, or it doesn't!"

After completing his theatre arts graduate program in 2008, Samuel detoured to Los Angeles. Having been a member of the long-running UCSC improv groups Humour Force Five and Someone Always Dies, he was eager to keep his skills sharp. "I ended up becoming a mainstage player at the Ultimate Improv theatre in Westwood," Samuel revealed. "During my tenure as a performer there, I was approached by JD Walsh, the owner of the theatre. He asked me if I wanted to be in a television pilot that he had written. I eagerly said yes, and we flew out to Wisconsin for a week of filming... I think I can speak without hyperbole that it was one of the greatest weeks of my entire life."

Samuel returned to UCSC in 2009 to begin his Ph.D studies in computer science. Walsh's pilot **Battleground** remained in limbo for a year and a half as it was shopped to networks. "There had been some screenings which had been well received, but other than that, the fate of **Battleground** was a complete mystery to me," Samuel noted. "One spring day, I received a phone call from JD letting me know that [streaming media website] Hulu was interested in picking up the show as their first original scripted programming." The show's fate was still tenuous, and Samuel learned that he would have to audition all over again. "Fortunately, all the miracles lined up! The show got picked up, I pleased enough folks at Hulu to win my part back (an honor which, sadly, not everyone from the original pilot holds), and I got to return to Wisconsin to film a thirteen-episode season."

Battleground documents the fictitious campaign of a dark-horse Senatorial candidate in the swing state of Wisconsin, focusing on her campaign staff. Samuel plays the idealistic young volunteer Ben Werner, who (like most viewers) is uninitiated in the world of campaigning. Does Samuel have much in common with his character? "I definitely try to approach everything in life with the same energy that Ben Werner does, and I'm certainly a little naive at times," Samuel admitted. "Ben Werner also develops a huge crush on fellow volunteer Lindsey Cutter, and I have more experience than I would care to admit having crushes on cute girls from afar."

Battleground is a landmark in Hulu's development, but Samuel is careful when discussing its place in the shifting world of new media. "Although the distribution of the show is on the web, the actual act of creating it was akin to filming a 'normal' television show," he said. "I firmly believe that there is a new type of medium that requires expertise in both the arts and the sciences to be able to produce, but I do not think **Battleground** is that medium." On the other hand, unlike some jittery mainstream networks, "Hulu really seemed to trust us to tell the story that we wanted to tell, in the way that we wanted to tell it." (At press time, there was no official word on the status of **Battleground**, though Walsh told **The Hollywood Reporter** in 2012 that a potential second season looks "positive." This state of limbo remains in summer 2014. Given the show's unusual production history, it's impossible to predict whether or not the hiatus will be permanent.)

Meanwhile, as part of UCSC's Expressive Intelligence studio, Samuel continues to work as lead engineer of the game **Prom Week**. In it, players control the actions of eighteen high school students during the week before their prom. Like high school itself, it sounds straightforward but plays out in an unpredictable, complex social system. The characters' functions required the team to create a new artificial intelligence system called Comme il Faut (CiF), which takes each facet of the high-school social state and reasons it over 5,000 rules of social and cultural considerations to determine what can happen next. Samuel enthused that "the system is maybe one of the strongest examples out there of a game that enables stories are a true collaboration between the programmers / authors, and the players / readers." He added that in preliminary analysis of more than 20,000 plays of **Prom Week**, it has taken players no more than four actions within the game to create a whole new story: "That's pretty exciting!"

In the end, Samuel's disarming enthusiasm rivals that of his television counterpart. "I'm very grateful that I've had so many chances to practice (and at times combine!) these two seemingly disparate facets of my life, and I can only hope that I'll have many more opportunities to do so in the future."

To learn more about **Prom Week,** visit promweek.soe.ucsc.edu. You can download and play the game at apps.facebook.com/promweek or search kongregate.com. The full first season of **Battleground** can be streamed at hulu.com.

SAMBADÁ

[From the Winter 2013 Student Guide]

The phrase "Brazilian music" conjures up a very specific sound in many people's minds: namely, the samba music that accompanies Rio's annual Carnaval. Yet, the country's diversity is reflected in a complex, unpredictable array of sounds. Brazil's cultural melange ensures a natural fusion of indigenous, African, and European rhythms and melodies. This is an alluring musical synergy in itself, but Brazilian musicians prefer to innovate instead of playing the same old song. For generations, they have been altering their musical foundation in any way they see fit. (Think of the Tropicália movement of the late 1960s, where the likes of Os Mutantes and Gilberto Gil tweaked psychedelia and rock while experimenting with Brazilian music, wittily subverting genre boundaries to form an intoxicating new sound.) What's more, their genius doesn't exist in a vacuum: as Brazilian musicians travel and settle throughout the globe, they find new sounds in their musical palette while imprinting their music onto the local landscape.

Santa Cruz's SambaDá perfectly embodies this musical legacy. While the band's lead singers are Brazilian-born, other members of the ensemble hail from such places as Bolinas, Sonoma, Los Angeles, and even Minnesota. Yet, the band came together in Santa Cruz, and has become a fixture of the city's concert scene over the years.

SambaDá percussionist Marcel Menard recalled the band's 1997 origin. "Some of us played live Brazilian percussion for the samba dance classes in Santa Cruz. Papiba [Godinho], our lead singer from Brazil, was teaching us rhythms of popular Brazilian samba music. After a few years we thought we should form a band." SambaDá's first gig at downtown's now-defunct Costa Brava was decidedly low-key and "so rootsy," according to

98

Menard. "We had one guitar and vocals through the same amp and a bunch of drums. But people loved it!" Frequent and rigorous rehearsals were the rule from that point onward, and the band's sound started to take shape.

Today SambaDá boasts nine members, many of whom play multiple instruments. While Menard credits co-lead singer Dandha Da Hora with adding "a real authentic Afro-Brazilian flavor" to the mix, other influences are less expected. For instance, saxophonist Anne Stafford, trained in jazz and ethnomusicology at UCSC and Cabrillo, also performs with a klezmer band. Will Kahn and Kevin Dorn each play bass, but Kahn loves hip-hop rhythms while Dorn is well-versed in salsa music. With such diverse elements, SambaDá's Afro-Brazilian foundation takes on a decidedly Santa Cruz accent. "We have created our own sound over the years that is hard to categorize," Menard asserted.

With nine personalities and scores of ideas in the musical mix, does this complicate SambaDá's songwriting? Menard revealed the band's creative process. "Usually our lead singers write lyrics and come up with a basic melodic idea, then the whole band adds their ideas and touches." He noted that for this "very democratic band," songwriting "definitely takes longer" but makes for "more interesting music" in the end.

A career highlight came in 2009, when SambaDá played shows in Brazil. The concert at the Senzala do Barra Preto in Salvador proved especially meaningful. "We played at the center [run by] Ilê Aiyê, the legendary Afro-Brazilian group and organization that fought for the rights of Black Brazilians to participate in the yearly Carnaval celebration in the '70s," Menard explained. "They are a beloved organization and carnaval bloco that represents the forefront of the social and human rights movement in Brazil, as well as a huge source of musical and cultural inspiration for all Brazilians and the global community." Dandha Da Hora had grown up performing with Ilê Aiyê, bringing the whole experience full circle. Menard noted, "I think that was a huge achievement for us and a special validation of how SambaDá bridges Brazilian and US culture."

SambaDá's latest album, 2010's **Gente!**, is its second collaboration with San Francisco-based producer Greg Landau. Having grown up in the Mission District, Landau played guitar with Latin rock bands before producing a diverse array of international musicians. Landau would seem to be a perfect fit for SambaDá, and Menard reflected on the Grammy winner's positive influence. "[He] pushed us to mix our music with various styles like funk, rock, hip-hop, and reggae as well as electronic sounds." You can stream audio or purchase downloads from all three SambaDá albums at sambada.com.

To supplement its demanding tour schedule, SambaDá plays public and private events alike. "Being a touring musician can be a hard life," Menard admitted, "but the rewards from performing and receiving energy back from our fans makes it more than worth it!" To book the band, contact Moshe Vilozny at (831) 421-2791 or realmoshe@yahoo.com.

SANTA CRUZ ART LEAGUE
[From the Spring 2013 Student Guide]

In a city considered the fifth most artistic in America by The Atlantic, it's difficult to imagine an arts organization flying under the radar. Most discussions of local exhibitions and First Friday Art Walks emphasize Pacific Avenue galleries and the Museum of Art and History, as well as the upstart Tannery Arts Center near Highway 9. Yet, tucked away on Broadway off Ocean Street, the Santa Cruz Art League has inspired and promoted the city's artistic growth for 94 years.

"We attribute the longevity of the Art League to an enduring need for artists to come together and share the mystery and beauty of their creative lives," noted T. Mike Walker, Art League board president. The organization started small in 1919, comprised of a group of local plein air artists who showed their work at what became the East Cliff Museum of Natural History. Led by museum caretaker (and the League's first president) Margaret Rogers, the group worked to establish its own home.

The Santa Cruz Art League incorporated as a nonprofit charitable organization in 1949. Art sales enabled the group to raise enough funds to purchase the current 526 Broadway property. Its gallery and theatre were constructed, and a classroom gallery was added later. Admission to exhibitions was always free, as a condition of the League's nonprofit status.

The turning point for the organization arrived in 1951, thanks to a life-sized replica of da Vinci's **The Last Supper**. Created by ceramicist Harry Liston and wax sculptor Katerine Stubergh, the sculpture graced the League's theatre stage through the late 1980s. More than two million visitors came to view the sculpture over the years, establishing the League's place in local art. (The sculpture was later given to the Odd Fellows for the Santa Cruz Memorial Park. Shown annually on Shrove Tuesday at the park, it can be viewed by special arrangement. Call [831] 426-2333 for details.)

As the League evolved, a sea change was brewing in Santa Cruz's art scene. Cabrillo College opened in 1959, and UCSC followed in 1965. "A new influx of young artists and ideas caused turmoil in the Art League, where traditional landscape & still life artists argued against including nude models or modern paintings," Walker revealed. When **The Last Supper** was removed, the theatre was opened to performances, adding dimensions of music and theatrical art to the League's offerings. A second, smaller gallery was added in the 1980s. Most importantly, the League's tiered membership hierarchy was dropped, expanding to include students and any supporters of the organization's programs. Today, nearly 600 people throughout Santa Cruz County are members.

The League continues to recognize and nourish new talent through its thirteen annual art exhibitions. Four of these are juried, offering more than $5,000 in prizes. **The Members' Exhibit** and the **High School Show** are annual standards, but it is the **Statewide California Landscape Exhibit** that has earned the most renown. Except for suspension during World War II, the **Landscape Exhibition** has run each year since it was established in 1928. It has a fascinating history of its own, having appeared at a variety of venues before the Broadway facility was established. The first one took place at the Santa Cruz Beach Boardwalk, and it was held on Treasure Island during the San Francisco World's Fair of 1939. The postwar era saw an annual stint at the Santa Cruz Civic Auditorium until the Art League's current home opened.

"How the SC Art Scene has evolved is encapsulated through the Art League, which has changed, struggled, matured and blossomed along with everyone else," Walker explained. "It's thrilling to be in the middle of such a rush of creative growth and activity. Santa Cruz has become like Paris in the 1920's—a hotbed of creativity in all of the arts—visual, written, dance, music, fusions of all sorts. Where once our gallery was one of a kind; now it is one out of many in our area." Naturally, the League is continuing to develop and innovate. The organization was recently given a series of theatre dates, which will be used for concerts, lectures, readings, and other special events. One goal is to establish a greater connection between the theatrical and artistic venues through First Friday events in the theatre, which will complement current exhibits. The League also leases its theatrical facilities to WEST Performing Arts Academy, who runs children's theatre camps and programs. Walker added that WEST "subleases space to some of the best improv groups in the country," making the venue's Broadway Playhouse influential in its own right.

"SCAL needs to evolve to grow into the 21st century," Walker asserted. "Younger members with vision and energy need to step forward and lead the group into the future. We are 94 years old and still dancing, but we need young artists with vision and energy to create whatever we wish to become." The public is invited to the League's meetings every third Thursday. Most importantly, Walker encouraged all Santa Cruz artists (students and professionals alike) to apply for all of the organization's juried shows. "Why not? Somebody's got to win them, and it might as well be you!"

The Santa Cruz Art League is located at 526 Broadway, off Ocean Street in Santa Cruz. Hours are 12 p.m. to 5 p.m. Wednesday through Saturday, 12 p.m. to 4 p.m. on Sundays, and extended hours through 9 p.m. every first Friday. For more information on classes and events, phone (831) 426-5787 or visit www.scal.org. For a schedule of performances at the Broadway Playhouse, phone (831) 425-9378 or visit www.westperformingarts.com.

THE WORLD AT YOUR EARS
[From the Spring 2013 Student Guide]

AZA

In a city that overflows with world music, Santa Cruz's Aza offers a complex, alluring melodic melange. Founders Fattah Abbou and Mohamed Aoualou originally hail from Morocco, both indigenous Imazighen people. (While Imazighen often are referred to as Berbers, they consider it a pejorative term.) They grew up playing traditional Tamzight (native Imazighen) music, as well as Gnawa (devotional music of the sub-Sahara) and various Arabic genres. Once the musicians moved to the US, they were inspired to fuse these traditions with a whole new array of sounds.

Abbou and Aoualou remain the linchpins of the band, composing and arranging most of the music. The lineup has changed somewhat over the years, due to various members moving out of town. The current incarnation produces sounds that go way beyond your average sextet, thanks to the instrumental versatility of all six members. While the band relies on traditional north African instruments such as oud (an Arabic lute) and bendir (a goatskin frame drum), everything from saxophone to penny whistle will find its way into the mix. Aza's first two albums are available at CDBaby.com, and both can be streamed at www.azamusic.com. [A third album, **Tayuga**, was released in 2014.]

In the midst of recording a third (more traditional) album, the band continues to play live shows, everything from local house parties to Bay Area jazz venue Yoshi's. Aza has toured nationally and internationally, but Abbou counts the band's Moroccan tours as particularly special. "It was the first time Aza played in front of 30,000 people in Festival Timitar [in] Agadir," he noted. "Also, it was an amazing experience to be able to give back the Moroccan public a music that was founded in their culture, in a different package."

Aza's influence continues to go beyond Santa Cruz's music scene. For several years, Abbou has been teaching Moroccan songs to a group of Santa Cruz students. By the time this article appears, he will have taken them to Morocco to perform publicly and collaborate with renowned local musicians. The students, in turn, plan to make a documentary about the trip. Abbou calls the project "an effort to bring the two cultures together, in these times where prejudice and fear of the unknown, fuels our clashes and pulling away from each other."

For more information about Aza, phone (831) 331-3849 or visit www.azamusic.com.

YUJI TOJO

For local guitarist and producer Yuji Tojo, the love of music started early. He began to play at the age of nine, delving into everything from jazz to rock to the traditional music of his native Japan. In the '70s he formed the band ETB, which followed grueling tour schedules throughout southeast Asia. The 1980s brought him to California, where he is now a fixture of Santa Cruz clubs and studios alike.

Tojo is an accomplished session and touring musician, working with everyone from country legend Lacy J. Dalton to the late Nigerian drum master Babatunde Olatunji. Since he knows both sides of the occasionally delicate relationship between producer and musician, he approaches his session work differently depending on his role. When he is a guest musician, he strives "to get the sound, tone, feel, closer [to the] producer's idea in the studio." On the other hand, while the producer Tojo tells musicians to do the same, he likes to "leave open space for them to be free at the same time," and let them incorporate some of their own inspirations.

While Tojo is comfortable exploring all sorts of musical traditions, he is not afraid to allow technological wizardry into the mix. He uses a Bose RC300 looping machine onstage to mimic multiple effects, everything from horn sections to the sound of raindrops. He is thus able to play with a stripped-down lineup at local clubs, making a two-piece sound like a full band. Of course, he points out, much of the success relies on the drummer involved onstage. "The drummer has to be able to hear the loop well. It's very important to make an accurate time loop; otherwise it will be a disaster because the drummer has to follow the loop. I am playing with drummers with a great sense of timing! Lucky!"

For the past few months, Tojo has been working on his upcoming CD. Since he is playing every instrument as well as producing, this as-yet-untitled album should prove to be his most personal project yet. "This CD is more groove-oriented with a pop and rock feel," he revealed. "It's very different than my previous one [2010's jazzy, Latin-inflected **Way of the Universe**]. I think I am more into simple stuff these days." You can find Tojo's music at such online vendors as CD Baby, iTunes, and Amazon, and stream his recordings at www.yujitojo.com.

Tojo plays at the Crow's Nest in Santa Cruz on the first and third Wednesday of each month, and frequently appears at such local venues as Zelda's, Paradise Beach Grille, and the Ideal Bar & Grill. He also plays house parties and private events. To book the guitarist (and receive up-to-date concert information), e-mail musashi@yujitojo.com.

SCULPTURE IS

[From the Fall 2013 Student Guide]

For five months of each year, Watsonville's Sierra Azul Nursery and Garden becomes strangely enchanted. The mayflies are made of bronze, and steel flowers bloom among the walkways. Oversized ceramic and glass pears exist alongside actual pear trees. Huge mobiles, abstract sculptures, and clever odes to nature delight the eye, and are nestled among two acres' worth of native plants that grow year-round. This unprecedented phenomenon, known to local art lovers as **Sculpture IS**, has returned for a seventh incarnation after a one-year hiatus.

In 2004, Pajaro Valley Arts Council board members Judy Stabile and the late Mary Warshaw were developing a gallery exhibition. "We were struck by the fact that we wouldn't be able to showcase larger pieces, because of the size of the gallery," Stabile said. When the two saw the imposing kinetic sculptures of Santa Cruz artist Moto Ohtake, they wanted to display several in the show. "[Ohtake] asked us how we would show his pieces so they would move. Of course, there was no way to do this at the gallery. So Moto was the inspiration for our desire to find an outdoor location in Watsonville that would serve as a 'satellite' exhibition."

The search began for a suitable location. Stabile drove past Sierra Azul Nursery and Gardens each day, and became convinced that the two-acre space could be the perfect venue. Neither she nor Warshaw knew anyone there, but talks with the nursery manager led to a meeting with owner Jeff Rosendale. Rosendale wholeheartedly approved. With a $6000 donation from Stabile's mother, Betty Heil, and additional funds from donors Warshaw found, the first **Sculpture IS** took root in 2006. The first edition was shown for seven and a half weeks, with Rosendale giving sculptors the option to keep pieces in the garden. (To this day, pieces are often "wintered over" from year to year.) The council, hoping to repeat the show's success, applied for and received a Community Foundation grant with plans to make it an annual event. Rosendale and Stabile would coordinate the project on a yearly basis.

The sheer scale of the procedure has forced some changes over the years. First, the curated exhibition evolved into a juried one. "Logistically, it would have been impossible, as volunteer curators, for us to spend the time visiting each of the artists' studios in a period of just a year," Stabile noted. Each year, the council sends out a call for artists, who submit digital images of potential submissions (or, occasionally, conceptual drawings for pieces yet to be made). Two or three jurors choose works based on quality of workmanship, durability, and scale in relation to the nursery garden. The show's scope has widened to include artists outside Santa Cruz County as well: featuring sculptors from as far north as Humboldt County, and as far south as San Luis Obispo County. Stabile notes that artists have started to work on site-specific sculptures, further enhancing the show's quality and reputation.

While far more sculptures can be presented in a two-acre outdoor setting than in a more traditional venue, the setting brings its own challenges. "The garden is family friendly, and we like to keep that in mind while selecting pieces," Stabile admitted. "The challenge becomes one of not censoring the work based on subject matter, yet providing an enjoyable experience for all of our patrons." The biggest concern is completely uncontrollable: weather. "If we have a particularly rainy season prior to installation (like our first year), it can be a challenge bringing in and setting heavier pieces," Stabile said. Since Sierra Azul is a fully functional commercial nursery, sculptures have to coexist with growing plants. "The pieces go into the garden in spring. When we place smaller sculptures, we have to be careful to place them so they will still be seen as plants grow up and around the pieces. The garden needs to be watered and mowed periodically, so sculptures must be able to withstand both the elements and garden maintenance."

Susana Arias has contributed to the show since its inception, co-curating the exhibition in 2009. When asked about the evolution of the exhibition, she illustrated how the show's novel setting provides unexpected benefits. "Houses are small in California," she pointed out, "but almost everyone has a garden. The [show's] outdoor setting has inspired more people to make, display, and buy sculpture locally without their being shackled to where to put it in the house." As a result, sculpture becomes a practical part of daily life in ways that people never considered. "A lot of people have been drawn more to sculpture, and sculpture collection, because of this exhibition," Arias stated.

Stabile stepped away from **Sculpture IS** in 2009 to curate other exhibitions. She continues to provide general mentorship for the venture, as well as big dreams for its success. "My hope is that the show will be profitable and continue to grow in both size and quality on an annual basis." She enjoys the show even more now that she is a visitor to the grounds. "**Sculpture IS** at Sierra Azul is a fabulous venue for California artists to show their work," she affirmed. "The garden that Jeff has nurtured over the years is a feast of colors and textures that changes with the seasons. The sculptures are the perfect companions to this extraordinary setting."

The Sierra Azul Nursery and Garden is at 2660 East Lake Avenue, Watsonville (off Highway 152, across from the fairgrounds). Admission is free, and hours are 9 a.m. to 5:30 p.m. daily. For more information, call (831) 728-2532 or visit http://www.pajarovalleyartscouncil.org/sculptureisatsierraazul.

REBIRTH OF THE COOL: AN ICE CREAM RENAISSANCE

[Adapted from the Fall 2013 Student Guide]

Within three years, Santa Cruz has become the unofficial ice cream capital of northern California. Legendary local firms continue to thrive, while upstart artisanal ventures have captured the city's imagination. How did this happen, given our relatively small population? Even the ice-cream makers themselves have no consensus. Some, such as Marianne's co-owner Kelly Dillon and Kelly Sanchez of Kelly's French Bakery, mention the year-round warm weather and tourist traffic. Others, such as Mission Hill's Dave Kumec and Polar Bear's Mary Young, feel it has more to do with the availability of high-quality local ingredients. Kendra Baker of The Penny Ice Creamery points to longtime support for food businesses, and Dillon's partner Charlie Wilcox credits educated Santa Cruz palates. At any rate, the following directory should help those willing to do some delicious research on the subject.

KELLY'S FRENCH BAKERY
402 Ingalls Street, Santa Cruz
(831) 423-9059
www.kellysfrenchbakery.com

While Kelly's has existed since 1981, it has only produced ice cream since 2010. Even so, ice cream is co-founder Kelly Sanchez's birthright. Her great-grandparents ran an ice cream shop in Los Angeles for decades, and her great-uncle attended Penn State's renowned Ice Cream Short Course in the 1920s. Sanchez had always experimented with ice cream at home, and in 2009, the renowned local baker attended the Short Course herself.

Sanchez's pastry expertise strongly influences her approach to ice cream. "I think that ice cream is perfect medium for sweets," she asserted. "I have always loved to make candy, so toffee crunch, caramel almond, and coffee brownie are common flavors that we make. I also make jam, so ollallieberry and strawberry ice cream are also on the list." Kelly's makes all its own inclusions (commonly nicknamed "mix-ins"), which is unusual in the industry.

When devising flavors, Sanchez is driven by her own palate. "We don't make any of the new savory / sweet flavors," she revealed. "I am a traditionalist this way. I like the classics, maybe with a little twist, but ice cream is a sweet treat to me. I never want to be challenged by the taste." Sanchez is particularly fond of the bakery's caramel almond flavor, which features her caramel almond brittle folded into caramel ice cream.

MARIANNE'S
1020 Ocean Street, Santa Cruz
218 State Park Drive, Aptos
(831) 458-1447
www.lovemariannes.com

Marianne's was established in 1958, quickly becoming a beloved fixture. While the company has had just one scoop shop for most of its history, it supplies ice cream to more than 300 restaurants, stores, and special events such as the Gilroy Garlic Festival.

Original owners Sam and Dorothy Lieberman, now in their eighties, sold Marianne's to Kelly Dillon and Charlie Wilcox in January 2013. "It's not [about] incorporating our vision into Marianne's," Wilcox asserted. "It's that Marianne's is the perfect vehicle for people who have a caring vision and want to have fun. That's the way Sam has always run it, and it suited us very well."

With all its commercial success, it is easy to forget Marianne's culinary influence. Marianne's has experimented with flavors for years, serving macapuno (young coconut) and black licorice long before unusual ice creams became trendy. The shop serves 75 flavors daily, and many are suggested by the store's 30 employees. One such flavor, a vanilla-based peanut butter and chocolate swirl called Heaven, has become a new standard, and a few more employee suggestions are being developed for introduction next summer.

MISSION HILL CREAMERY
1101B Pacific Avenue, Santa Cruz
(831) 216-6421
www.missionhillcreamery.com

Before opening Mission Hill Creamery in 2010, Dave Kumec spent years in the tech industry, managing content and marketing for such companies as LightSurf and VeriSign. Prior to that, the France-trained chef had managed restaurant crews for EuroDisney Resort (now Disneyland Paris). It's no wonder that Kumec was drawn to ice cream, since it's the perfect melding of creativity and science. Mission Hill's original scoop shop was located on Front Street, and reopened on Pacific Avenue in September 2012. While the retail location was closed, Mission Hill developed a loyal, still-expanding wholesale clientele, including several natural-foods chains and the Monterey Bay Aquarium.

Kumec's approach is influenced by nearby farmer's markets and their exceptional produce. "I learn what is at peak ripeness...My culinary training helps me to treat these products properly, and to preserve the fresh, wonderful flavors in the form of ice cream and sorbet." Customers clamor for Mission Hill's salted caramel, inspired by the classic version at Berthillon in

Paris. Ever the purist, Kumec prefers vanilla bean, "the perfect flavor for all occasions."

THE PENNY ICE CREAMERY
913 Cedar Street, Santa Cruz
820 41st Avenue, Santa Cruz
(831) 204-2523
www.thepennyicecreamery.com

Co-founder Kendra Baker first gained acclaim as a pastry chef for restaurants such as Michelin-starred Manresa in Los Gatos. There, she became intrigued with ingredients sourced from local farming and foraging communities. Cherished memories of secret ice-cream parlor trips with her dad inspired her to take on the challenge of making ice cream that incorporates these ingredients.

The combination of nostalgia and novelty leads to powerful experiences on both sides of the counter. Baker loves the moment when a customer first steps away from chocolate and vanilla (which, she hastened to add, are always available) to try something new: "Seeing their face light up as they enter a whole new world of flavor exploration is a real treat." To Baker, strawberry pink peppercorn best embodies Penny's approach. Featuring locally-sourced Dirty Girl strawberries, "it's a party in your mouth."

POLAR BEAR
389 Coral Street, Santa Cruz
(831) 425-1108
www.santacruzpolarbear.com

Polar Bear opened in 1975, delighting local fans ever since. Former Cafe Cruz manager Mary Young made the ultimate show of devotion, buying the business once original owner Carolyn Gray retired. "I always wanted to own my own business, and we served Polar Bear at the restaurant," Young recalled. "Here I am over seven years later." She oversees the small-batch production of more than 100 flavors, as well as custom-made ice cream cakes, mud pies, and novelties. A successful boutique line of flavors, exclusive to legendary Santa Cruz candy store Marini's, was developed in 2008. Polar Bear is most renowned for its Mexican chocolate flavor, Young noted: "People love it, and come from all over to get it."

POSTSCRIPT: Original Marianne's co-owner Sam Lieberman passed away in November 2013 at the age of 84. In happier news for the company, Marianne's Aptos location opened in June 2014. Kendra Baker and Zachary Davis added a full-service sit-down restaurant, Assembly, to the Penny's growing empire; it opened in March 2014.

Regular **Student Guide** readers may recall that this article first appeared under the title "The Rebirth of Cool." At the time I was very upset that the Miles Davis reference **Rebirth of the Cool** was inexplicably changed, and no one gave me a convincing reason why it happened. So, I have restored my original jazzy title here. Revisionist history for the win!

UP TO SCRATCH: SANTA CRUZ DJS
[From the Winter 2014 Student Guide]

From street-corner busking to performances in nightclubs, Santa Cruz is synonymous with live and acoustic music. It may surprise you to find that the DJ club scene thrives in all corners of Santa Cruz County. The sounds being spun are as exciting as those coming from the local stages, blending genres and breaking boundaries. You're about to meet a few of the minds behind the music, and hear their opinions about everything from mashups to the local scene. Then, you'll get some tips on where to find your new favorite groove.

THE VETERAN: DJ MARC
Lifelong music lover Mark Peterson played the violin and drums in his youth, hoping for a career in television or radio. The self-proclaimed "parent, grandparent, and cook" doesn't fit most people's mental profile of a DJ, and he resisted the calling for a while. What changed his mind? Credit the US military. "My army buddy bought some equipment," he confided. "He let me practice a bit, and I caught on fast."

In the beginning, Peterson played soul, r&b, and hip-hop exclusively. When he started to spin at raves, he added house music to the mix. His style continues to evolve. "I scratch less now," he noted, mentioning a fondness for more "quick mixes and mashups." Known as DJ Marc, the formerly reluctant DJ has residencies at two local clubs. He plays '90s music every Tuesday night at the Blue Lounge in Santa Cruz's Seabright neighborhood, and presents dance music and theme nights Fridays at downtown Santa Cruz's Blue Lagoon.

THE GENRE-BREAKER: DJ SHEA BUTTER

For Shea Modiri, sound was an irresistible force. "From a young age, I was blessed to have an Irish mother who woke us up on Sundays playing Santana...loudly. I always knew early on, I'd be involved with music." Everything clicked into place when he discovered records. "I guess the moment when I first bought vinyl, I was hooked," he said. As DJ Shea Butter, Modiri blends all eras of soul with reggae and hip-hop, favoring rarities while throwing a few hits into the mix.

The vinyl fanatic has made a nimble transition to the digital age. He has mixes available for streaming and download at SoundCloud, which can also be reached via his page at djsheabutter.tumblr.com. Yet, it's the BVMO Music collective, found at bvmomusic.com, that fuels his passions. "I'm motivated by those within my community that inspire me to push the boundaries," he explained. "I've developed unique relationships that continue to craft my passion in an art that is becoming so easy to 'manipulate.'" Find him at the Red in downtown Santa Cruz every first Friday, as well as at the Twitter and Instagram handle DJSheaButter.

THE GOTH GURU: DJ AMP PYRE

A longtime member of the local goth and industrial scene, the "very shy" Terry Mendoza didn't spin records until a year and a half ago. "It was one of those things that I wanted to do...I remember the energy and the people that were out there dancing to my first set. From that point on, I fell in love and have been doing this ever since." DJ Amp Pyre is now a linchpin of the Box (the Blue Lagoon's Sunday goth night), and hosts the Wicked Lounge every first Saturday at the Blue Lounge.

The newcomer began with old school goth, electronic body music, and industrial, but has branched out in recent months, citing fellow Box DJs and former resident DJ Stats with the inspiration. "I see myself as teachable, meaning that I am open to hear what is new out there," Amp Pyre explained."I don't want to be that kind of person that thinks that knows it all, and I don't. As long as I remain humble and [do] not have an ego, I will continue to do what I love to do."

THE TECH SPECS

Those who love old-school rap smile at the thought of a DJ equipped with two turntables and a milk crate full of vinyl records. Yet, today's DJ culture goes hand in hand with digital recording. Companies such as Serato have created relatively inexpensive consoles and programs, allowing DJ to alter sounds, sync beats, and even (virtually) scratch using a computer.

Yet, the romance of vinyl is hard to give up. DJ Marc is a recent convert to digital DJ software. "I was the pioneer who refused to change, but my age caught [up] with me," he confessed. "[The equipment] got too heavy!" What does he enjoy about the new digital format? "It has gotten a lot easier to set up and use," he noted, mentioning that it offers "a lot of options that are much easier...[than] just trying to do it on two turntables. And I will say this again: it's a hell of a lot LIGHTER!"

Other DJs enjoy the best of the analog and digital worlds. "I still use two turntables and a mixer," DJ Shea Butter confided. "The only change has been from vinyl to Serato [to] save me a ton of back pain from carrying record crates." The newfound ease of mixing made him fall in love with the process all over again. "When I was younger, before the Serato era, spinning records was more of a hobby," he attested. "Years later, it's my life."

THE MASHUP: FAD OR FOREVER?

Mashups are new recordings formed when multiple songs are blended and altered into a single track. The idea itself isn't new: the Timelords' 1988 single "Doctorin' The Tardis" (which hit #1 in the UK and New Zealand) mashed up the **Doctor Who** theme with several British glam-rock classics. Even the Beatles' "Revolution 9" technically fits the genre. Nevertheless, the ease and economy of digital mixing has contributed to the current mashup explosion. But as anyone traumatized by the unholy union of Burt Bacharach and the Scissor Sisters on TV's **Glee** can attest, they're not easy to do well. What is the secret, and are mashups just a novelty?

DJ Marc increasingly relies on mashups, and finds the fuss understandable. "It's a new style, so everyone wants to do what's new." The key, he feels, is to choose songs with care, explaining that "a good ear for music" is paramount. "If you match music and songs right, it will sound good."

"I love them!" proclaimed DJ Amp Pyre. "I think they are becoming popular simply because they are fun if done right." Pyre is more of a mashup fan than practitioner, having witnessed the downside of the genre. "I heard some mashups that were...not great. I don't do them personally because I am not quite there [yet], but I'll throw some ideas to [DJs] and let them see if it will work or not."

While DJ Shea Butter agreed with the fun involved, he pointed out that a mashup has science added to its art. "It's comparable to a puzzle: putting things together that match, that blend just right." This touch of mystery provides intrigue for the DJ and listeners alike. "I've always enjoyed it," he affirmed. "There're some gems out there."

FELLOW DJS AND THE AUDIENCE

Since DJs take such pride in their work, you might expect the competition to be cutthroat. It's heartening to discover that the community seems to be fairly close-knit. DJ Amp Pyre credits a "great crew," including fellow resident DJs Morphobic and Ash, with musical and emotional support, calling it "one big happy and close family."

Santa Cruz's geographic location means that clubgoers nurture local talent, while discovering DJs visiting from San Francisco and the South Bay. This works both ways, since all of the DJs interviewed perform in other parts of the Bay Area. DJ Shea Butter revealed, "I've driven from San Jose to San Francisco to Santa Cruz back to San Jose in one night for gigs because this is what I love." He welcomes the diverse tastes of the Santa Cruz audience: "It allows me to take chances and throw in some curve balls throughout the night."

The music-savvy population of Santa Cruz is a boon to local clubs, but it can be a double-edged sword for the DJs who play there. "For the most part, there are a lot of barstool DJs" in Santa Cruz, according to DJ Marc. "They feel that they are entitled to hear whatever they want, regardless of the advertised genre of the night." Having spun music in venues from San Francisco to San Luis Obispo, he found patrons there more respectful: "They know it's entertainment and a job." His heartfelt advice rings true for enthusiastic newbies and those who feel they've heard it all. "Just realize that DJs are human beings and we do our best to entertain," he said. "To some of us it's a job and a livelihood, and sometimes people forget that. If you like to ask for a song, BE POLITE! Rudeness gets you ignored!"

A sympathetic audience can make all the difference, behind the mixing table and in life. "The Box has a special place in my heart because it isn't just a great club, but I use it as one of my support systems. I have been clean and sober for eight years and let me say, if it wasn't for those people, I wouldn't be here today," DJ Amp Pyre insisted. "They have such great respect for my sobriety and that is why I love them. Now my Wicked family is the same thing to me."

JUST GET ME TO THE DANCE FLOOR!

If your heart is set on a particular genre, you'll have a favorite DJ or club theme night in mind. On other nights, you may feel musically open-minded, or just want to hang out in a certain neighborhood. You're bound to find intriguing sounds wherever you go. But where do you go? The list below may not be definitive (since the scene is always evolving), but should get you started on your musical odyssey. If you're under 21, you should check first to see if you're allowed in to a particular event. Even if the venue is an all-ages restaurant before 10 p.m., the laws can be tricky after hours.

THE BLUE LAGOON
923 Pacific Avenue
Santa Cruz CA 95060
(831) 423-7117
www.thebluelagoon.com

THE BLUE LOUNGE
529 Seabright Avenue
Santa Cruz CA 95062
(831) 423-7771
www.thebluelounge.com

MARGARITAVILLE
231 Esplanade
Capitola CA 95010
(831) 476-2263
www.margaritavillecapitola.com

MOTIV
1209 Pacific Avenue
Santa Cruz CA 95060
(831) 429-8070
www.motivsc.com

RED RESTAURANT AND BAR
200 Locust Street
Santa Cruz CA 95060
(831) 425-1913
www.redrestaurantandbar.com

ROSIE MCCANN'S
1220 Pacific Avenue
Santa Cruz CA 95060
(831) 426-9930
www.rosiemccanns.com/santacruz

ZELDA'S ON THE BEACH
203 Esplanade
Capitola CA 95010
(831) 475-4900
www.zeldasonthebeach.com

STAR WARS: WHERE SCIENCE MEETS IMAGINATION

[Originally published as "The Force Is With Them," in the Winter 2014 Student Guide]

In 1977, filmmaker George Lucas debuted **Star Wars** to a clamoring public. Decades later, the saga of "a galaxy far, far away" still ignites our collective imagination. Many have pointed to its classical storytelling and vivid characters as its secrets to success, relegating its technological advances to flashy window dressing. Yet, as the story has encompassed multiple films and reached new generations, its high-tech wizardry has influenced the scientific community, not just Hollywood. This intriguing concept is explored in the traveling exhibition **Star Wars: Where Science Meets Imagination**, making its final stop at San Jose's Tech Museum of Innovation through February 23, 2014.

Curated by Boston's Museum of Science and the still-unbuilt Lucas Cultural Arts Museum, the exhibition features models, costumes, and props from all six **Star Wars** movies. While there are plenty of impressive structures on display, Lucas and his crew place surprising emphasis on everyday moments and objects in their work. Lucasfilm still uses physical models in spite of the prevalence of computer-generated imagery, since it's easier for crew members to gather around a model than an image on a computer monitor. Lucas frequently invokes the "used universe design philosophy" in his creations, making some objects in the movie universe look old, repaired, or repurposed-- just as they would in everyday life.

Several sections show how seemingly fanciful **Star Wars** societies take direct inspiration from past and present human populations. In 1980's **The Empire Strikes Back**, life on the ice planet Hoth seems risky and frightening. Yet, as the exhibition explains, humans often settle in similarly inhospitable areas for various reasons (such as scientific research), and are forced to adapt. Elsewhere, parallels are drawn between Kashyyk (the home planet of Chewbacca) and tropical rainforests on Earth. Some Star Wars environments, such as the entirely artificial world of the planet Coruscant, reflect potential realities of the future, provoking thought and debate.

While the **Star Wars** films draw inspiration from life, they often foreshadow our technological advances. This is especially clear in the "Robotics Today" segment of the exhibition. Our society still lacks thinking, feeling robots such as C-3PO and R2-D2, but so-called "social robots" improve our daily lives in fascinating ways. Relatively common droids such as the iRobot Roomba vacuum cleaner are shown alongside such wonders as the Huggable Therapeutic Robot. First created in 2005, the Huggable features a full-body "skin" equipped with touch sensors that respond to tactile stimulation. This makes the Huggable an option for patients who would benefit from a pet but have health issues that prevent them from keeping one. While robots are used for the common good, the exhibition also explores the ethical issues involved in artificial intelligence. If robots ever become sentient beings, how will robot rights be acknowledged in comparison to human rights? Just as in the **Star Wars** movies, no clear-cut answer is given.

The exhibition employs interactive sections to establish connections between the fantastic **Star Wars** creations and their emerging real-world counterparts. Take the Engineering Design Lab, where museum visitors can combine magnets with Lego bricks to build magnetized cars that float above a track. The models are reminiscent of the landspeeder vehicles in the Star Wars films, but also explain the ideas of magnetic levitation (where objects are suspended by magnetic fields) and electromagnetic propulsion (the emerging concept of vehicles that move solely through the propulsion of magnetic forces). This area is rounded out by the "Real World Speeders" display, introducing viewers to such promising prototypes as the Moller Skycar M400 and Boeing's Canard Rotor/Wing prototype from 2003. While more than 2.8 million people worldwide have seen the exhibition at its previous nineteen stops, The Tech promises several unique events to end the tour memorably. On January 19, "Droids and Tales From The Set" will feature Industrial Light and Magic special effects artist Don Bies in conversation with radio host Angie Coiro. Industrial Light and Magic visual effects artists and model makers Kim Smith and Carol Bauman will speak with Coiro on February 16, in a program fittingly titled "The Star Wars Women." Hands-on science workshops will take place throughout the show's run, and the museum will extend its hours during selected "Jedi Nights." At once accessible and breathtaking, the Tech Museum's incarnation of **Star Wars: Where Science Meets Imagination** will delight everyone, not just film fanatics and science buffs.

The Tech Museum of Innovation is located at 201 South Market Street in San Jose. For information on ticket prices and special events, phone (408) 294-8324 or visit www.thetech.org.

HIDDEN HEROES: THE GENIUS OF EVERYDAY THINGS
[From the Winter 2014 Student Guide]

Many people would not think that the coffee filter has much in common with adhesive tape, or that the paper clip has anything to do with the canning jar or bubble wrap. Yet, according to Germany's Vitra Design Museum, these objects share several important characteristics. Based on ingenious yet easily understood ideas, they have become daily staples of our lives while remaining virtually the same over decades. Coining the phrase "hidden heroes" for these and many other items, the museum created a touring exhibit to pay proper tribute to these unsung doodads. From now through February 2, 2014, viewers can discover **Hidden Heroes: The Genius of Everyday Things** at the San Jose Museum of Art.

To the uninitiated, the exhibition sounds like a cold tribute to the mechanical takeover of our lives. Happily, the most low-tech gadgets get the most enthusiastic treatment in **Hidden Heroes**. Seemingly obsolete objects as the incandescent light bulb and the ring binder are extolled in the label texts. Furthermore, the simplest pieces receive the most striking presentations. In a clever multimedia display, the evolution of earplugs is revealed. From their first mention in Homer's **Odyssey** through their appearance in the World War I trenches to today's use by industrial workers and music-hungry concertgoers, their trajectory is unexpected. "I was surprised at how compelling the earplugs were to me, because you don't really think about [them] that much in 2013," admitted Kat Koh, curatorial assistant at the San Jose Museum of Art. "But before industrialization, things were much quieter. There weren't trains, or buses, or cars everywhere, or jackhammers. There was no need for earplugs. Just the fact that earplugs were invented shows that our society was going forward technologically."

Most museum exhibition websites are little more than an afterthought. In contrast, the Vitra's site at www.hidden-heroes.net has won no fewer than 28 creative awards since its 2010 debut. Through a stylish and user-friendly interface, online visitors can choose among 44 objects to create over a thousand individual versions of the exhibition. While this is a boon for those wanting to know more, does it detract from the exhibition's physical presence in San Jose? "I think what the website does is provide flexibility, another option for people," Koh replied. While Koh affirmed that a lot of the information on the site is identical to what's presented in person, viewers will miss the layout and color of the presentation boxes, as well as the chance to interact with them. Instead, she preferred to think of the Vitra's site in another way. "Many exhibitions come with a book that is published alongside [the] lifetime [of its run]," she noted. "So, the website for **Hidden Heroes** sort of serves as an e-exhibition catalog."

The San Jose museum imprints its own stamp on the exhibition through its interactive interpretation area. Here, viewers are introduced to the idea of upcycling, where the **Hidden Heroes** objects are revealed to have intriguing potential. "These objects were chosen for their staying power, essentially," Koh explained. "Most of them haven't changed since they were invented. But, people are constantly finding new and contemporary ways to use objects." Shipping containers, with their sturdy construction and standardized sizes, are shown to make useful architectural material. Most compelling is the UNICEF Brick prototype, designed in 2011 by the South Korean firm Psychic Factory. The UNICEF Brick appropriates the shape of Legos, featuring two round compartments that can be filled with relief materials such as rice or soil. The bricks can lock securely when they're stacked, effectively forming temporary shelter. "When I saw that," Koh enthused, "I thought it was such a great use of an object that's been around since the early 20th century, just reconceptualizing it as a humanitarian aid tool."

Koh points out that there are many different versions of the story of these objects, and visitors can discover them through the exhibition labels. "Certain objects tell the story of modernity," she noted. "Another version you can play is 'Find The Cousins.' Bandages and adhesive tape are closely related; paper clips and clothespins use the same principle of elasticity to work." The Post-It Note is just one of the featured objects created by mistake, adding an appropriate feeling of serendipity to the proceedings. "It's really interesting, all the different narratives you can come up with in the show," Koh said. "I'm constantly finding new ones, too."

The San Jose Museum of Art is located at 110 South Market Street in San Jose. For information on admission fees and special events, phone (408) 271-6840 or visit www.sjmusart.org.

CUTTING HER OWN PATH
[Adapted from the Spring 2014 Student Guide]

The Museum of Art and History honored papercut artist Nikki McClure with her own exhibition through May 25, 2014. McClure received her science degree from a college renowned for its progressive philosophies, verdant landscape, and odd mascot. While the school in question is Evergreen State College in Olympia, Washington and not UC Santa Cruz, the museum's staff considers McClure a perfect match for our city. "We wanted to have this exhibition to showcase an incredibly talented artist but we also felt that the stories, themes and concepts of her work connect deeply to the values in our Santa Cruz community," noted Stacey Marie Garcia, the museum's director of community engagement. "The MAH and Nikki have similar philosophies in that we believe through art, stories can be shared that can inspire common connections across many differences. We believe her work has the power to bring about those connections."

Since McClure is self-taught as a papercut artist, her art is marked by unusual influences, such as her study of natural sciences at Evergreen. "During that time [McClure] was training her eye to see nature's details, forms, movements and shapes," Garcia explained. "This later helped guide her hand in translating those observations into art. She did a lot of technical drawings in her science classes and studied entomology intensely, spending almost entire weeks drawing a single fly." At the same time, McClure's unusual papercut method (using a single sheet of paper per image) embraces chance as well as exactitude. "She sees mistakes as an opportunity to experiment," Garcia said, "and often finds that through that exploration she arrives at some of her favorite pieces." Her work tends to emphasize themes of community, celebrating a father teaching his child to skateboard or families washing dishes and mending clothes.

McClure's unique ethos is reflected not only in her craft, but in the ways her work is sold. Patrons may have noticed her calendars and notecards for sale at Bookshop Santa Cruz. McClure's work has been a mainstay of the independent web storefront buyolympia.com, a four-person operation that has flourished since 1999. For Garcia, the grassroots distribution reflects the ethos of Olympia's music scene. "[McClure] began by publishing her own books at Kinko's, photocopying and stapling each page and then hand coloring them in," she noted. "These DIY methods reflect the cut-and-paste, photocopied zine aesthetics that were used to distribute the feminist politics of the [early-to-mid-1990s] Riot Grrrl movement." By emphasizing independent and local distribution, McClure's commercial success has proved not only inspirational but helpful to other artists.

If McClure's approach is more reminiscent of an indie musician than a visual artist at times, this is no coincidence. She was first drawn to Olympia for its music scene in the early '90s, and immediately flourished there. Not only has McClure designed shirts and cover art for bands such as Sleater-Kinney, but she has released music herself. McClure appears on several 7-inch singles and compilations released by stalwart Olympia labels K Records and Kill Rock Stars. Music even informs her work process; as she told Garcia, "Music helps to carry me [through] the knife cutting. It makes it a dance of my hand and body." Visitors were able to listen to McClure's musical influences as they examine her work in the show.

Several special events took place at the museum to celebrate the McClure exhibition. A Third Friday theme of poetry and book arts was featured on March 21, where visitors learned about bookbinding, paper making, and altered books. The artist herself spoke with patrons on April 4, and on April 5 McClure led visitors through the gallery, revealing personal stories about her work and process. This unprecedented openness has endeared Santa Cruz to the artist and her disarmingly personal body of work.

The Museum of Art and History is located at 705 Front Street in downtown Santa Cruz. For admission fees and other information, phone (831) 429-1964 or visit www.santacruzmah.org.

NATIONAL DANCE WEEK SANTA CRUZ
[Adapted from the Spring 2014 Student Guide]

For one brief yet remarkable week in late April, strange and wondrous phenomena occur in Santa Cruz. Ordinary citizens become mavens of mambo, barons of the ballroom. Their exuberance escapes local dance halls and studios to take over unusual venues. (I once witnessed a group of young women dressed in full Brazilian Carnaval regalia, complete with feathered headdresses, dancing the samba down the aisles of a local supermarket.) Finally, they will assemble en masse to dance in the streets. That magical time is known as National Dance Week Santa Cruz.

National Dance Week began in 1981, through a grassroots movement by dance-related organizations wanting to bring greater recognition to the art form. Abra Allan, owner of Santa Cruz dance studio Motion Pacific, noted that Dance Week has had many local incarnations over the years, with different artists at the helm. Allan began presenting National Dance Week Santa Cruz in 2008. "I believed strongly that Dance Week should be a vehicle for bringing dance to the community and taking it out of the studios and theaters and bringing it to the streets."

While the event has grown exponentially in the past few years, "the event really was significant from year one," Allan said. She credited the strong history of local collaboration with the event's broad scope and success. "Dance Week has worked in collaboration with the [Museum of Art and History], Santa Cruz Fringe Festival, First Friday Santa Cruz, UCSC, Cabrillo College, and many local dance studios," she explained. "The event now presents over 200 dancers and is witnessed or participated in by over 4,000 community members."

Perhaps the most beloved Dance Week mainstay is Dance In Unlikely Places, which presents dance in very specific yet untraditional sites. "From crosswalks to bus stops, bridges to buildings, dancers and choreographers are reshaping our conventional ideas about performance," Allan enthused. She noted that the location becomes as much a part of the performance as the dancers themselves. "Brought out into the world, dance expands its imaginative repertoire, engages with new audiences...These are the moments that catch people by surprise and really bring a smile to people's faces as they move through their day at the local grocery store, bookshop, or even just crossing the street downtown."

Dance In Unlikely Places produced Allan's favorite memory of Dance Week thus far, which happened in 2008. "Mir & A Company, a local contemporary dance company, created a pop-up dance in Bookshop Santa Cruz," Allan recalled. "The patrons in the bookstore were so excited that a couple dozen of them ran all over the bookstore following this company of dancers as they moved through the space. It was like watching children explore. They were so joyful!" This year's edition will include a specially-commissioned piece by nationally renowned choreographer Dixie Mills, involving the Downtown / Beach Trolley. "The rest will have to be a surprise," Allan replied mysteriously.

Allan is eager to remind readers that Dance Week gives them a great opportunity to experience dance, not just witness it: "Through Open Classes, you can take a first dance class, come back to dance after many years, or try a new kind of dance." Hundreds of classes will be offered at dozens of locations throughout the county. "With no excuses and nothing to lose, dancers from beginner to advanced can shake it up in any number of free classes offered throughout the week."

For a full National Dance Week Santa Cruz schedule of events, visit santacruzdance.com. Motion Pacific is located at 131 Front Street, Suite E, Santa Cruz. Phone (831) 457-1616 or visit motionpacific.com for more information about classes and facilities.

2001: A KITCHEN ODYSSEY
[From the August/ September 2008 Moxxi]

It started innocently enough. My parents were finally getting their kitchen remodeled, and the work had just begun. On the first day, my mother surveyed the proceedings for a while, then
approached me with concern. "I think I might serve the workers some coffee and snacks. What do you think?"

I eyed her warily. Knowing my mother, today's innocent plate of cookies would evolve into an increasingly complex parade of dishes in the coming weeks. To make matters worse, these Lucy-and-Ethel schemes would invariably involve me somehow. I thought it over.

"Go ahead. Just don't stay awake nights worrying about what the foreman takes in his coffee." As she headed to the kitchen, I had no idea that I had just set a ritual in motion which, within six months, would grow to take over our lives.

It's hard to pinpoint exactly where things went awry. Most of the time, the workmen graciously took all foodstuffs in stride. Nevertheless, my mother's combination of culinary prowess and fierce pride soon became her downfall. After all, how could she serve a packaged cookie—or nothing at all—when she had presented everyone with a beautifully arranged fruit plate the day before?

Her duty was clear. In the days that followed, she would serve cinnamon toast, small egg salad sandwiches, cheese and crackers, even quesadillas. Drawn into her web, I found myself contributing homemade chocolate-chip cookies and blueberry muffins to the cause. Apple juice was provided for those who didn't like coffee, and soda was available in the afternoon (Coke and Pepsi, to avert any potential Cola War distress).

How was this done, you ask? We created a makeshift kitchen setup using a twenty-year-old Maxim convection oven and two hot plates. The convection oven worked surprisingly well, though its small size precluded preparation of turkey dinners or a side of beef. The hot plates, on the other hand, were more temperamental. Sometimes they would turn chicken breasts to charcoal within five minutes. Usually, we could have enjoyed a full tasting menu at the French Laundry in the time it took to boil water.

My mother, galvanized by her successes and the prospect of more mouths to feed, grew more ambitious. She would take remarks such as "Kitchen remodel? Bet you're eating a lot of takeout!" as a grave insult. Eager to prove that she could cook well without a kitchen, she frequently invited people over for dinner. My father and I stopped grumbling after a while, realizing that we were powerless foot soldiers in the shadow of General Patton.

I can only imagine what went through our guests' minds. My father would usher hapless visitors in quickly and ply them with drinks. Yet, I am fairly sure that no matter how loudly he regaled them with stories about vintage cars and elderly Yugoslav immigrants, they could still hear the frenzied culinary efforts going on in various rooms, punctuated by exchanges like these:

"Where are the steaks?" (My mother would try to keep her tone light, disguising the anxiety in her voice for her visitors' benefit.)

"They're on a cookie sheet by the bathtub," I would reply wearily.

"Where's the salad bowl?"

"I just told you. It's on your bed!"

In spite of this, or perhaps because of it, my mother's reputation for hospitality continued to grow. Lighting technicians, electricians, and city inspectors would come for the project, but stay for the food. The pressure mounted as our patrons grew to expect a certain standard of service. ("I don't understand," the contractor's assistant lamented one day. "She's a half-hour late. The coffee ALWAYS comes out at 9:30.") We finally realized things had gone too far on the morning my mom walked into the addition to find a stranger drinking coffee and reading the paper.

"The other garbage men have been talking about this woman who serves food to all her workers," he informed her. "I didn't believe it, so they told me to stop by."

Mom just shrugged and topped off his coffee mug.

Eventually the project ended, and now those frenetic months seem increasingly distant. The struggle to fry an egg is easily forgotten when one is newly blessed with multiple gas burners. Even so, I would like to think that the experience gave me new perspective not just on food preparation, but on my family's wacky sense of solidarity. Tonight, I just might fire up the hot plate and invite the whole clan.

CPSIA information can be obtained at www.ICGtesting.com
Printed in the USA
LVOW08s2003180615

442868LV00001B/35/P

9 781632 634665